15 Ways to Live Longer and Healthier

Life-Changing Strategies for Greater Energy, a More Focused Mind, and a Calmer Soul

Joel Osteen

Nashville New York

ALSO BY JOEL OSTEEN

15 WAYS TO LIVE LONGER AND HEALTHIER
15 Ways to Live Longer and Healthier Study Guide

ALL THINGS ARE WORKING FOR YOUR GOOD
Daily Readings from All Things Are Working for Your Good

BLESSED IN THE DARKNESS
Blessed in the Darkness Journal
Blessed in the Darkness Study Guide

BREAK OUT!
Break Out! Journal
Daily Readings from Break Out!

DIGEST BOOKS
Believe
Stay in the Game
The Abundance Mind-set
Two Words That Will Change Your Life Today

EMPTY OUT THE NEGATIVE
A Fresh New Day Journal

EVERY DAY A FRIDAY
Every Day a Friday Journal
Daily Readings from Every Day a Friday

FRESH START
Fresh Start Study Guide

I DECLARE
I Declare Personal Application Guide

NEXT LEVEL THINKING
Next Level Thinking Journal
Next Level Thinking Study Guide
Daily Readings from Next Level Thinking

PEACEFUL ON PURPOSE
Peaceful on Purpose Study Guide
Peace for the Season

PSALMS AND PROVERBS FOR EVERYDAY LIFE

RULE YOUR DAY
Rule Your Day Journal

THE POWER OF FAVOR
The Power of Favor Study Guide

THE POWER OF I AM
The Power of I Am Journal
The Power of I Am Study Guide
Daily Readings from The Power of I Am

THINK BETTER, LIVE BETTER
Think Better, Live Better Journal
Think Better, Live Better Study Guide
Daily Readings from Think Better, Live Better

WITH VICTORIA OSTEEN
Our Best Life Together
Wake Up to Hope Devotional

YOU ARE STRONGER THAN YOU THINK
You Are Stronger than You Think Study Guide

YOU CAN, YOU WILL
You Can, You Will Journal
Daily Readings from You Can, You Will

YOUR BEST LIFE NOW
Your Best Life Begins Each Morning
Your Best Life Now for Moms
Your Best Life Now Journal
Your Best Life Now Study Guide
Daily Readings from Your Best Life Now
Scriptures and Meditations for Your Best Life Now
Starting Your Best Life Now

YOUR GREATER IS COMING
Your Greater Is Coming Study Guide

15 Ways to Live Longer and Healthier

Cover design by Micah Kandros
Author photograph by Matthew Daniel

FaithWords
Hachette Book Group
1290 Avenue of the Americas, New York, NY 10104
faithwords.com
twitter.com/faithwords

First Edition: October 2023

FaithWords is a division of Hachette Book Group, Inc. The FaithWords name and logo are trademarks of Hachette Book Group, Inc.

The publisher is not responsible for websites (or their content) that are not owned by the publisher.

The Hachette Speakers Bureau provides a wide range of authors for speaking events. To find out more, go to hachettespeakersbureau.com or email HachetteSpeakers@hbgusa.com.

FaithWords books may be purchased in bulk for business, educational, or promotional use. For information, please contact your local bookseller or the Hachette Book Group Special Markets Department at special.markets@hbgusa.com.

Library of Congress Cataloging-in-Publication Data
Names: Osteen, Joel, author.
Title: 15 ways to live longer and healthier : life-changing strategies for greater energy, a more focused mind, and a calmer soul / Joel Osteen.
Other titles: Fifteen ways to live longer and healthier
Description: First edition. | Nashville : FaithWords, 2023.
Identifiers: LCCN 2023020948 | ISBN 9781546005087 (hardcover) | ISBN 9781546006404 | ISBN 9781546006763 | ISBN 9781546006770 | ISBN 9781546005100 (ebook)
Subjects: LCSH: Mental health—Religious aspects—Christianity. | Stress management—Religious aspects—Christianity. | Success—Religious aspects—Christianity.
Classification: LCC BL65.M45 O884 2023 | DDC 248.8/62—dc23/eng/20230602
LC record available at https://lccn.loc.gov/2023020948

ISBN: 9781546007890 (TBN edition)

Printed in the United States of America

LSC

Printing 1, 2023

CONTENTS

INTRODUCTION

After one of our services, I met a man who looked to be in his seventies. It came as a surprise when he told me he was over one hundred years old. It wasn't just that he was as handsome or as healthy looking as could be that threw me off. It was that he was so full of joy, his mind was sharp, and he had been having such a good time with everyone around him. He stood in the line nearly forty minutes waiting to visit with me. I told him we could have pulled up a chair for him so he didn't have to stand.

"I don't need to sit down," he said with a big grin. "When I get old, I'll sit down."

"I can't believe you're that old," I said. "You don't have a wrinkle on your face."

"Joel," he replied, "I just don't crack." Then he told two or three more jokes. We laughed and laughed. When he walked away, he turned around and said to everyone, "I'll see you next year."

I fully expect God will give him another year. I thought to myself that in his one hundred years, he'd had lots of troubles, had people hurt him, and made mistakes, but he was still young at heart, full of faith and energy. It was no wonder he seemed so healthy, so happy, so strong. He had a great sense of humor and loved to laugh. It made me think about all of God's natural healing that had been released and flowing in him all those years.

God created us to live a healthy, abundant, joyful, faith-filled life. He destined us to be confident, to be free, to be positive, and to be happy. He didn't create us to drag through the day, to be worn out by problems, discouraged and depressed by disappointments, even sick physically because we're living so stressed out, uptight, and worried. But it's easy to get so focused on what's wrong in our life, what we don't have, and how big our obstacles are that we leak out our joy and passion for living.

I know some people who actually get depressed every Monday morning. They don't like their jobs, they dread going to work, and every week, they develop a bad case of the Monday Morning Blues. Oddly enough, in several studies of various populations over the years, researchers have found that deaths from heart attacks occur at their lowest rates on weekends, jump significantly on Mondays, then drop again on Tuesdays. Most researchers blame the stress of returning to work on Monday for the increased risk.

My father believed that the world would be a healthier place if we stressed less, laughed and enjoyed life more, and learned the habit of emptying out any offenses, hurts, regrets, and condemnation. He never lost his youthful spirit. He knew that prolonged stress can damage your health and significantly shorten your life. He knew that when people are uptight and on edge, headaches, digestive problems, high blood pressure, and lack of energy are just some of the results. They don't sleep well. Much of this would go away if they learned how to deal with stress.

Scientists have shown that if you go through life in a negative frame of mind, uptight and stressed out, always worried, full of fear, carrying emotional wounds and past guilt, your immune system will weaken, making you more susceptible to sickness and disease. Studies have shown that negative emotions actually weaken the production of the natural killer cells that our immune system creates to attack and destroy abnormal cells that cause disease. On the other hand, people who are happy and have a positive outlook develop more natural killer cells than the average person. When you stay full of joy, your immune system functions at its peak performance level, just as God intended. You'll increase your brain activity and creativity, which can help you overcome challenges in difficult times. You'll reduce the stress hormone and increase production of the human growth hormone, also known as the "youth hormone," which slows down the aging process and keeps you looking younger and fresher. The Bible says, "A cheerful mind works healing," and that Scripture continues to be confirmed by science.

The psalmist says that "joy comes in the morning." Every morning God sends you a fresh supply of joy. Every day is a gift to be vibrantly alive, to live it to the full. He has given us everything we need to live healthy and whole, but we have to do our part and tap into the promises of God and those things that breathe new hope into our heart and new vision into our spirit. We can't let wrong mind-sets, a negative past, and other people's opinions discourage us from experiencing all the good things God has for us. I believe it's your time to walk in the fullness of His blessing.

In this book, you will discover fifteen life-changing strategies for more energy, vitality, and happiness. We'll explore how to:

- *Have a healthy soul*
- *Stay positive toward yourself*
- *Deal with difficult people*
- *Let go of control*
- *Choose to be happy*
- *Live in the present*
- *Tame the tongue*
- *Take care of yourself*

I know these strategies work, because they've worked in the lives of my family members, friends, and associates, as well as in my own life. As you read these pages, be open to what God will reveal to your heart. I'm confident that if you will take these steps with me, you will be happier, healthier, and you'll rise higher than you ever imagined possible—not just for a week, or a month, but for the rest of your life.

CHAPTER ONE

A Healthy Soul

Your inner life is more important than your outer life.

We spend a lot of time and energy taking care of our physical body. We try to eat right, exercise, get enough sleep, and take vitamins. That's all important. We want to feel good. But we don't spend enough time taking care of our soul. We don't realize how much our emotions, our attitudes, and our thoughts are affecting us physically. The Scripture says, "I wish above all things that you succeed and be in good health, even as your soul prospers." This links being healthy physically, having energy and vitality, to how healthy your soul is. If your soul is unhealthy, it's going to spill over to the physical.

If you're living stressed, worried, bitter, guilty, and angry, those negative emotions are not just affecting your relationships, your creativity, and how productive you are. They're weakening your immune system. Your cells are not fighting off sickness as they should. I've read that 90 percent of all visits to a primary care physician are stress-related. You can't sleep at night, your food won't digest, and you have ulcers. Much of that goes back to your soul not being healthy. You're worried night and day about your child who's off course, stressed over your finances, and holding a grudge over a friend who did you wrong. You don't realize that you're making yourself sick. All that negative energy is poisoning your soul. Because your soul is unhealthy, it has spilled over to the physical.

You wake up in the morning and wonder why you're still tired, why you don't have any energy. It's because your mind worked all night. Your body lay there, but your mind wrestled, wondered, and reasoned. You thought, *What if...? How can I...? What may happen...?* You're trying to control things that you can't control. You're trying to fix people who you can't fix. You're worried about a problem that may not even happen. You're bitter over something that took place twenty years ago. You can't take in all those toxins and not be poisoned. You can't let anger, unforgiveness, guilt, and worry dominate your life. If you get your soul healthy, you'll get your energy back. If you quit letting the negative emotions rule, many of these physical ailments will go away. It's all interconnected.

> *If you get your soul healthy, you'll get your energy back.*

Pay Attention to Your Inner Life

In my late twenties, I developed a redness between my eyes and all around the top of my face. It made my skin flake, was very itchy, and looked so bad. I tried creams, lotions, and different facial soaps, but nothing improved. I went to dermatologists who gave me prescriptions that helped control and lessen it, but it never went away. A couple years went by, and finally I went to a different doctor. He said, "I know exactly what's causing this. It's stress. You're living too uptight. You have too much pressure. I can give you more medication, but until you change, until you get more balanced, it's not going to go away." I was young and had so much energy. I thought, *I'm not under stress. I'm fine.* Sometimes we can't see what's poisoning us. We have a blind spot. We look in the mirror and see a physical problem. We see the redness, or the blemish, or that we need to lose some weight. But we can't see what's happening inside. Your inner life is more important than your outer life. What's going on in your emotions, how you feel about yourself, and what you're allowing to play in your mind are affecting what's happening on the outside. I was treating the symptom but not the cause. I thought, *Just fix the outside. Just clear this redness up.* But it kept coming back.

What's going on in your emotions, how you feel about yourself, and what you're allowing to play in your mind are affecting what's happening on the outside.

One day I got honest with myself. I considered everything I was doing and my commitments. I was married to Victoria, which was incredibly...relaxing. We had a two-year-old son, with another baby coming. We had moved out of our townhouse and were remodeling an older house. I had traveled several weeks to India with my father. I was working long hours at the church, trying to get the TV ministry going. I didn't realize the level of stress and pressure I was living under. Much of it, I was putting on myself. I like to go fast, work hard, and accomplish goals. But here's a key: You are responsible for your own emotional well-being. It's not up to anyone else. Your spouse can't keep your soul well. No one, including your doctor, your friends, or your parents, has control over your soul except you. In one sense, not even God has that control. He's not going to make you forgive someone or make you not worry. He's not going to force you to not live angry, offended, stressed, and guilty. Those are choices we have to make.

My question today is, Is your soul healthy? We can see your looks, your talent, and your personality. But what's going on inside? Are you at peace? Are you turning things over to God? Do you know that you're valuable? Is your heart free from bitterness and offense? Or is there worry, guilt, insecurity, and self-pity? "Look at what I've been through. I'm so angry. I have this chip on my shoulder because they hurt me." That's poisoning your soul, but if you're like I was, you may not be able to see it. Sometimes we've gotten used to these negative emotions. We've adapted. Then we wonder why we don't have energy, why we can't sleep, why we're not creative. You have to get honest with yourself. You have to look inside and ask, "Why am I jealous? Why can't I celebrate my friend's success? Why am I easily offended? Why do I argue so much? Why don't I feel good about who I am?"

Is your soul healthy?

A lady told me that every time she and her husband had the smallest disagreement, she would come unglued, blow up, and get loud. It would turn into a huge ordeal. Her husband couldn't understand why she was so on edge, so easily angered. Over time, it had become too much and their relationship was falling apart. What he didn't know was that as a teenager, she had been in a relationship with a young man who hurt her deeply. When he had suddenly broken up with her, he said some things that were very derogatory. She felt rejected, not good enough. Instead of letting go of that offense, knowing that God is our vindicator, that what people say doesn't determine who we are, she held on to it inside. It was poisoning her spirit, making her insecure and easily offended. When you don't let go of hurts and emotional wounds, they never heal. Any time her husband didn't agree with her, it was like touching a bruise. She would push back and lash out. One day she did what we all have to do. She got honest with herself. She looked inside and asked, "Why am I like this? Why do I get upset so easily?" She realized it was from the pains of the past, from things that weren't fair that she had never dealt with. She made the decision to get rid of the unforgiveness, the bitterness, the resentment. That was the turning point. As she got her soul healthy, her relationship became healthy. Today, she and her husband are happy and enjoying life.

Pay attention to your inner life. It's easy to adapt to things that are poisoning us and we don't realize it. We end up going through life just treating the symptoms. If we get to the root cause and get our soul healthy, God says we will have good health and good success. We need to ask ourselves: "Am I making myself sick? Am I sabotaging my relationships? Am I limiting my potential, holding myself down because my soul is unhealthy?"

It's easy to adapt to things that are poisoning us and we don't realize it.

Get Rid of the Roots

The writer of the book of Hebrews says, "Make sure that no root of bitterness springs forth and defiles you." It describes bitterness as a root. You can't see a root because it's underground. But if you let it grow, it's going to spring forth. A bitter root will produce bitter fruit. What's inside is going to show up on the outside. We try to fix the fruit. We deal with the symptom, but the fruit is not the problem. We need to go to the source and get rid of the root.

Proverbs says, "Guard your heart, for out of it flows the issues of life." One of our main responsibilities is to keep the toxins out.

If your soul is bitter, your life will be bitter.

Keep those roots from springing up. Offenses are going to come. Cranky coworkers will come. You can't stop disappointments, hurts, jealousy, and anger from coming. The question is, Are you going to let it take root, get down in your spirit, contaminate your joy, steal your peace, take your energy, and open you up to sickness, trouble, and defeat? No, keep your soul healthy. You have to be an active gardener. Pull up those roots. Pull up the unforgiveness. Pull up the insecurity. Pull up the guilt and condemnation. Don't let your soul become poisoned. If your soul is bitter, your life will be bitter. If your emotional well-being is contaminated, it's going to affect your physical well-being.

Why are you letting that worry take root, then losing sleep and living stressed out? You've seen God take care of you in the past. You've seen Him make ways where you didn't see a way. You've seen Him provide in a pandemic, give you peace in a storm, favor in the fire. He did it back then, and He's going to do it again. He didn't bring you this far to leave you. Why are you holding on to that guilt, beating yourself up over past mistakes? God has forgiven you, so why don't you forgive yourself? God doesn't remember it, so why don't you quit remembering it? God has moved on, so why don't you move on?

Why are you jealous over the coworker who got a promotion or over the friend who you think is more beautiful, more talented, more successful? Now you're finding fault, being critical, feeling bad about who you are. God blessing them doesn't mean He's not going to bless you. God didn't run out of favor. He didn't forget about you. He has things in your future that are better than you've imagined. Don't let that jealous root keep you poisoned. Pull it up. Keep your heart pure. Celebrate their success. When your soul is healthy, God can trust you with more.

Why are you still upset over what happened twenty years ago? Why are you still holding a grudge over someone who hurt you and walked away? Why are you angry about what someone didn't give you? That didn't stop God's plan. What they did is not going to keep you from your purpose. God knew it was going to happen, and He already had a plan to bring you out better, to give you beauty for the ashes, joy for the mourning. Pull up that root of disappointment, resentment, and self-pity. That's poisoning your future. That's limiting your potential, draining your energy, and weakening your immune system. Don't just deal with the symptom; get to the root. Learn to live from a place of faith. "God, I trust You. I know You're in control. You're fighting my battles. You're ordering my steps. You have a good plan for my life. You're my provider, my protector, my way maker, my vindicator, my deliverer. God, my life is in Your hands." That's how you keep your soul healthy. On a regular basis, you have to pull up roots, get rid of toxins, and guard your heart.

Don't just deal with the symptom; get to the root. Learn to live from a place of faith.

You Control What's in Your Soul

There was a man who owned a stable of horses. One day when he was out riding his horse, he saw a large tree limb had fallen across the trail. His horse went to jump over it but didn't quite clear it, and the horse scraped one of its back legs very badly. The man took the horse to the barn and cleaned the wound, put some antiseptic on it, and wrapped it up. A couple of weeks later, he noticed the horse was still bothered by it. The veterinarian came and looked at the wound and put the horse on antibiotics. The horse began to improve, but a few months later the infection returned, and his horse could barely walk. They started another round of the same antibiotics, and the wound began to heal. But three months later, the wound was reinfected. The owner finally decided to take the horse to the clinic and get a better evaluation of what was going on. The horse was put under anesthesia, and the veterinarian opened up the wound. He found a chunk of wood about the size of a golf ball buried way up in the horse's leg. That's why every time the horse went off the antibiotics, the infection came back. They were treating the symptoms, but until they went deeper, until they got to the root of the problem, it wasn't going to go away.

We treat symptoms because we can see the symptoms. It's obvious. "My skin is red and flaky. I need some medication." But we have to go deeper. We have to deal with the root. "I can't get rid of these headaches because I'm so worried, so stressed. I'm making myself sick." "I can't get along in this relationship because I'm insecure. I don't feel valuable." "I'm not reaching my potential because I'm mad at myself. I'm living in regrets, thinking about where I should be." Get the infection out. As long as the root is there, the fruit is going to be bitter. The good news is that you control what's in your soul. You can't control what happened to you, what someone did or said, but you can control how you respond, what you choose to dwell on, and what your attitude will be. Is there an infection in your soul and some toxins that are keeping you from getting well physically? Is there some bitterness, worry, anger, or guilt that is keeping you stuck, that is keeping you from flourishing?

> *Is there an infection in your soul and some toxins that are keeping you from getting well physically?*

Sometimes we can't get along in relationships because we have a root of pride. We think we're right all the time. We won't listen to other people's opinions. We won't apologize. We're hard to get along with, contentious, touchy. Pride is one of those toxins we can't always see. You have to look deeper, under the surface, to find it. When your soul is healthy, you're loving and kind. You see the best in others. You're a peacemaker. You let them be right.

Get Honest with Yourself

In Psalm 119, the psalmist says, "God, keep me from lying to myself." That is one of the most powerful prayers we can ever pray. "God, help me to be honest with myself. Help me to look inside and see where my soul is not healthy. Help me to see where I need to change, where I need to forgive, where I need to be more kind and understanding. Help me to see where I need to quit letting people take my joy, where I need to get over what happened three years ago, where I need to quit beating myself up for mistakes I've made. Help me to see myself as valuable, as attractive, as a masterpiece." My prayer is, "God, don't let us go through life lying to ourselves." It's one thing to be dishonest with others, which is certainly not good, but don't lie to yourself. Don't sweep things under the rug, make excuses for why you're angry, bitter, jealous, and hard to get along with. There's no fault in being there today, but there is a fault in staying there. It may be your explanation, but don't let it be your excuse.

> *"God, don't let us go through life lying to ourselves."*

"Joel, I have this ongoing infection because I scraped my leg." Get the wood out and move forward with your life. "I'm bitter

The Scripture says that you will have success and good health as your soul prospers.

because my loved one died." No, pull up that root, let the grieving process work, and go out and do great things. Make your loved ones proud by leaving your mark. "I'm stressed because of my finances, my children, and the pressure at work." You can't control all that. Don't let circumstances be an excuse to live worried, on edge, and to be short with your children. Get back in balance. Life is too brief for you to live that way. Get your soul healthy. If you look inside and deal with things that are stealing your peace, taking your joy, and causing you to compromise, then as your soul gets healthier, physical healing will come. Your gifts will come out in greater ways, your relationships will be better, and new doors will open. The Scripture says that you will have success and good health as your soul prospers. Notice there's a requirement. God says, "If you want success, good health, good relationships, and abundance, then do your part and keep your soul healthy—your attitude, your thoughts, and your emotional well-being."

It's interesting that most scholars believe that David wrote Psalm 119 and that prayer about not lying to himself. Maybe it stemmed from the time when he had an affair with Bathsheba. His army was out fighting a battle, but he stayed back in the palace. One night he went on the rooftop to get some fresh air, and he saw this beautiful woman taking a bath. Instead of walking away and not going there, he went and got his binoculars. Even though Bathsheba was married to one of David's faithful soldiers, he sent for her. When she ended up getting pregnant, David

The problem with burying negative toxins is that they never stay buried.

tried to cover it up. He had her husband, Uriah, come home from the battle, but Uriah was so loyal that he refused to sleep with her while his colleagues were out fighting. So David told the commanders to put Uriah on the front lines and then withdraw any protection from around him. Uriah was killed in the battle. David took Bathsheba as his wife, thinking that everything was fine. He covered it up, which didn't seem like a big deal. But the problem with burying negative toxins is that they never stay buried. Those toxins will eventually come back up and poison your life.

For the next year, while David was lying to himself about what he'd done, pretending nothing was wrong, his health began to deteriorate. He was sick and weak. Here he'd been strong his whole life. He was a warrior, but now his soul was unhealthy. The guilt, the shame, and the compromise started to affect his physical body. He finally got honest and admitted what he had done wrong. In Psalm 51, he said, "God, forgive and cleanse me from my sin. Create in me a clean heart." He was saying, "God, I'm not hiding anymore. I'm going to deal with these toxins that are poisoning my soul." The beauty of our God is that He's merciful. He'll forgive you. God restored David. He got his health back, his joy back, and he went on to fulfill his purpose.

But until you get honest with yourself and deal with what you know is holding you back, you're going to be limited. As your soul gets healthier, your body is going to get healthier. You're going to have more energy and vitality. David also wrote in Psalm 23, "He restores my soul." Your soul may feel broken, wounded, hurt from mistakes you've made or from what someone else did. But your soul can be restored. When you get honest with yourself, you release what you need to release—the guilt, worry, anger, jealousy—and then healing will come. Joy will come. Peace will come. I believe that even now God is working to restore your soul. Emotional healing is taking place. Healing from the hurts, the

> *Your soul may feel broken, wounded, hurt from mistakes you've made or from what someone else did. But your soul can be restored.*

pains of the past, what wasn't fair, the loss, the heartache. Healing from self-inflicted wounds, mistakes you've made, regrets you're living in. Healing from tormenting spirits, from mental illness, from anxiety and depression. God is doing a new thing. Forces that have held you back are being broken off your emotions, your attitudes, your thoughts. You're not to live wounded. He's restoring your soul. Your latter days are going to be better than your former days. You're about to step into a new level of joy, peace, fulfillment, abundance, and victory. Don't believe the lies that it's too late, that you've made too many mistakes, that you've been through too much. No, the best part of your life is still in front of you.

Get the Poisons Out

When I was growing up, our family knew a man who loved to play the piano. He was very talented, but he suffered from rheumatoid arthritis. Over the years, his condition kept getting worse and worse. All his joints were swollen. It got to the point where his fingers were so bent over that it looked as though he was making a fist. He couldn't open his hands up, and he couldn't play the piano anymore. He had loved to play for hours, but now that dream was gone, leaving him so discouraged. One day he heard my father talking about how important it is that we don't hold on to hurts and how unforgiveness can poison our life. This man suddenly felt convicted for something he had held against his parents for years, feeling they had done him wrong. Instead of letting it go, showing them mercy, he had let that bitterness take root. He had shut them out of his life, refusing to speak to them. He thought that was the best way to handle it. He didn't realize that was poisoning his soul. When your soul is unhealthy, it can affect you physically. That day he made the decision to forgive his parents and make things right. When he went to see them, his mother wept with joy and his father was so happy. It was an answer to their prayer. This man said that as he forgave his parents, he felt a heavy weight lift off him. He had gotten used to it. He had forgotten what it felt like to be free, to not have that bitterness in the back of his mind, always poisoning his joy.

It was great that his parents wanted the reconciliation. They were happy to have their son back. But there may be times when the people who did you wrong don't want to reconcile. They don't want to have you in their life. That's okay. You're not forgiving for their sake; you're forgiving for your sake. Forgive so you can keep your own soul healthy. Let it go, so that negative root doesn't spring up and contaminate the rest of your life. They hurt you once, but don't let them continue to hurt you by holding on to it. Let God be your vindicator. He sees what wasn't fair. He knows who did you wrong. And He knows how to make it up to you. He knows how to bring you out better than you were before.

Forgive so you can keep your own soul healthy.

Over the next few months, much to this man's surprise, his fingers started opening up little by little. The swelling started to go down, and he got better and better. A year later, he could sit down and play the piano as though he'd never missed a beat. It's amazing what can happen when our soul gets healthy. When we get free from the bitterness, the guilt, the stress, the worry, and the anger, that's when healing is released. That's when you'll see good success, the blessing of God in new ways.

Joy Is Medicine

I realize that not all sickness is from a lack of emotional well-being. But any time you face sickness, you're going to have to be strong in your emotions and in what you allow to play in your mind. When my mother was sick with cancer, she wrote letters to people who she thought she may have offended, asking them to forgive her. She was making sure that no toxins were in her spirit, that nothing she had done was poisoning her emotional well-being. She knew the emotional will affect the physical. She even watched cartoons and funny television programs that would make her laugh. The Scripture says, "A merry heart is like taking medicine, being joyful brings healing, but a broken spirit dries up the bones." If you go around discouraged, defeated, and saying, "Look at this medical report. I'm never going to get well," you're helping that sickness. You're giving it life. But when you're cheerful, when you know God is in control, when you're thanking Him when you could be complaining, when you're laughing when you could be crying, that's sending healing to your body. I believe many diseases will go away—headaches, high blood pressure, digestive problems—when we start taking our medicine by laughing, being joyful and good-natured.

> *"A merry heart is like taking medicine, being joyful brings healing, but a broken spirit dries up the bones."*

We focus a lot on the outside, but I'm asking you to look inside. Is your soul healthy? Are you spending your day being positive, hopeful, and grateful, or are you weighed down with stress, burdens, and worry? How can you be creative when you're using so much energy for the negative? How can your immune system work properly when you have bitterness, anger, and regrets? How can you be the mother, the father, or the leader you're called to be when you have toxins poisoning your spirit? It's time to get honest with yourself. Don't go another year letting something that you have control over to hold you back. Get your soul healthy. Pull up those bitter roots. Start turning things over to God. Release the worry, the hurt, the disappointment over what didn't work out. Keep your heart pure. If you do this, I believe and declare that because your soul is healthy, you're going to have good success and good health. New doors are about to open, opportunity is going to find you, healing is coming, with strength, energy, and vitality.

CHAPTER TWO

Stay Positive Toward Yourself

Nobody should think better of you than you.

Do you realize that the most important relationship you have is the relationship you have with yourself? Too many people don't like who they are. They focus on their faults and weaknesses. They relive their mistakes and failures. They wish they were different. They wish they were taller, had a better personality, or looked like their cousin. Instead of accepting themselves as a masterpiece, made in the image of God, they're critical toward themselves. Then they wonder why they're not happy and why they don't have good relationships. It's because they don't like themselves. If you don't get along with you, you're not going to get along with other people.

Jesus says, "Love your neighbor as you love yourself." You can't love others if you don't first love yourself. The best thing you can do for your family and friends is to be good to you, be kind to you, be merciful to you, be forgiving to you, be loving to you. You're good to others, so why aren't you good to you? You don't criticize your friend, so why are you criticizing you? You

> *You can't love others if you don't first love yourself.*

compliment your coworker, so when was the last time you complimented yourself? You admire other people's talents, so why don't you admire your talents? Start being good to you. That's not being selfish or arrogant; that's loving yourself.

Too many people go through life being against themselves, feeling as though something's wrong inside. I heard someone say, "I discovered the enemy. It was me." Are you your enemy? Are you defeating yourself, limiting your dreams, sabotaging your relationships—all because you don't like yourself? You have enough people and circumstances against you, so don't be against yourself. When you wake up in the morning, don't lie in bed and think of everything you feel is wrong with you or what you don't like about your looks, and don't relive your mistakes. *Why didn't I finish college? I should have been more disciplined. I lost my temper yesterday.* Those are toxic thoughts that will drain your strength, your energy, and your enthusiasm. Instead of focusing on what you think is wrong with you, start focusing on what's right with you. You have weaknesses, you've made mistakes—we all have—but there's a lot more right with you than there is wrong with you. Dwelling on the negative doesn't help you to do better. Beating yourself up for past mistakes doesn't move you forward. The better you feel about yourself, the better you'll do. The more you like yourself, the further you'll go.

You can't give away what you don't have. If you're in turmoil inside, critical of yourself, feeling angry and condemned, that's what you have to give. If you're hard on yourself, you'll be hard on others. If you don't forgive yourself, you won't forgive others. If you don't get along with you, how can you get along with your family? The best thing you can do is start being for you. When you love yourself, you can love others. When you're kind to yourself, you can be kind to others. It starts with you.

> *You can't give away what you don't have.*

Approve Yourself While You're Changing

Perhaps you're saying, "But, Joel, I have all these faults, these weaknesses. Once I overcome them, once I learn to control my temper, be more disciplined, and quit saying things I shouldn't, then I won't be down on myself." If you're waiting to perform perfectly before you feel good about who you are, you'll be waiting your whole life. You have to accept yourself while you're in the process of changing. God knew you would have weaknesses. He made you. You're not a surprise to Him. He's not sitting on His throne in heaven, scratching His head and thinking, *I didn't see that coming. They're a mess. What am I going to do?* He knew the things you would struggle with. You're not supposed to beat yourself up because you haven't arrived yet. I don't know one person who has arrived. There will always be some area in which we need to improve.

In fact, I believe that God will leave weaknesses in our lives on purpose, so we have to depend on Him. He's changing you from glory to glory. Learn to enjoy the glory that you're in right now. You may not be where you want to be, but you're not where you used to be. Instead of looking at how far you have to go, you need to look back and thank God for how far He's already brought you. It takes a mature person to say, "I'm okay with where I am while I'm on the way to where God is taking me."

It takes a mature person to say, "I'm okay with where I am while I'm on the way to where God is taking me."

One time someone asked me what the one thing was that I would change about myself if I could. I don't mean to sound arrogant, but I couldn't think of anything. Sure, there are plenty of areas in which I need to improve. I need to change and to grow. My point is that my weaknesses are not on the forefront of my mind. I'm not focused on my shortcomings, reliving my failures, or down on myself for past mistakes. I know that I'm forgiven, I'm redeemed, I'm a masterpiece, and I'm made in the image of Almighty God. Life is too short for you to go through it being against yourself. I say this with humility: "I like myself. I like my looks. I like my personality. I like my sense of humor. I like my taste of things. I like my physique. I like who God made me to be."

It's very powerful when you can say you like yourself. It's not, "I'll like myself after I lose twenty pounds, after I learn to keep my mouth closed, or after I become more patient." God accepts and approves you right where you are—faults, mistakes, shortcomings, and all—and not when you overcome all that, but right now. He knows you're on a journey. He's changing you little by little. He accepts you; now you have to accept yourself. He approves you; now you have to approve yourself.

It's very powerful when you can say you like yourself.

Focus on the Right Images

When our son, Jonathan, was fourteen years old, he and I were out playing basketball one day. We had played one-on-one for many years. I could always beat him, but he kept getting bigger, stronger, and better. It was on this day that he beat me for the first time. I played hard, did my best, but he won. I gave him a high-five, then I told him he was grounded. Though I lost, I had had some great moments during that game. At one point, Jonathan got around me and went up for a shot. I came from behind, timed my jump perfectly, went up with all my might, and blocked his shot. I felt like LeBron James as I swatted the ball into the bushes. It would have been an ESPN SportsCenter Daily Top 10 Play.

A few days later, we were in the gym playing basketball with some other guys. Jonathan said, "Dad, tell everyone what happened last week." I said, "Oh, yeah, Jonathan beat me to the hoop and went up for a shot, but I timed my jump perfectly and blocked it." He said, "No, Dad. Tell them about how I beat you." The funny thing is that the defeat wasn't on the front of my mind. That failure wasn't taking up the most space. It was my victory, my accomplishment, my success that stood out. It's all in how we train ourselves. Some people are focused on their losses, their flaws, their mistakes, and the times they didn't measure up. That's why they're negative toward themselves. The wrong images are always playing in their mind.

You need to focus on your victories, to focus on the times when you succeeded, when you resisted the temptation, when you were disciplined. You need to focus on the time you felt like telling someone off, but you bit your tongue, or when you went the extra mile at work, or when you excelled on a presentation. Don't let the negative take up the most space. You can't become who you were created to be if you're negative toward yourself. Yes, there are forces trying to stop us, but I wonder if you are your own enemy. Circumstances may be against you, and people will come against you, but you can overcome those things. The problem is if you are against you. If you're negative toward yourself, that can keep you from your destiny.

You need to focus on your victories, to focus on the times when you succeeded, when you resisted the temptation, when you were disciplined.

Your Gifts Fit You

God has given us different personalities, different temperaments, and different gifts. Sometimes we're fighting who we are when we're trying to be like someone else. You have to accept who God has made you to be. Sure, there are areas in which we can improve and grow, but there are certain things that make us who we are. I'm naturally quiet and reserved. My personality is laid-back, easy-going. I don't lose my temper. I seldom get upset. That's all natural to me.

When my father went to be with the Lord, I knew I was supposed to step up and pastor the church, but I didn't feel qualified. I had never ministered, and I didn't have the training, but I could get past those things. What I struggled with was that my father had a strong personality. He was dynamic and forceful. I saw other ministers who were loud and excited their audiences. I thought, *I don't have those strengths. I can't minister like them or my father.* When we compare and think we have to be like someone else, we can feel shortchanged, as though we're at a disadvantage. *I'm not as talented as they are. I can never be like that.* Here's the key: God has given you what you need to fulfill your destiny. If you needed a different personality, He would have given you one. If you needed different gifts, different strengths, different looks, or different parents, it would have happened. Quit comparing yourself to others and run your own race.

I was tempted to feel inferior, not strong enough, not good enough. I had to tune all that out and use what God had given me. I discovered that my gifts fit me. My personality, my talent, my strengths, and my temperament are right for my assignment. I didn't have to be loud, dynamic, or forceful like my father was. That worked for him, that's who he was, but God makes us

> *You have to be comfortable in your own skin, comfortable in who God made you to be.*

individuals. You have to be comfortable in your own skin, comfortable in who God made you to be. Don't covet what someone else has. If you had their gifts, their personality, or their looks, it wouldn't help you; it would hinder you. You are equipped for your race. You have the right personality, the right gifts, and the right looks. You're the right height, and you come from the right family. You weren't shortchanged, and you're not at a disadvantage. You have been fearfully and wonderfully made. Walk in your anointing, be confident with your gifts, and let your personality shine. There's not another person in this world like you.

The enemy would love for you to go through life trying to be an imitation, copying someone else who you think is more attractive, more gifted, more successful. No, be you. Nobody can do you like you can do you. You're not anointed to be someone else. The anointing on your life—the favor and the blessing—is to be you. You won't activate the favor, and you won't see the abundance, if you're trying to be someone that you're not, feeling wrong inside because you're not like someone else.

> *Nobody can do you like you can do you.*

Is Your Weakness Really Your Strength?

When I stepped up to minister, I wasn't like my father. What I thought was a weakness, being more calm and laid-back, was actually a strength. People started watching and attending our services in record numbers. Half of the people who watch our services say they've never been to church and never listened to a minister on television.

I wonder if you're fighting what makes you unique. Are you frustrated over what you think is a weakness, when in fact it's a strength? Quit wishing you were different and step into who God made you to be. He didn't accidentally give you the wrong personality or the wrong gifts. He didn't make you too quiet or too outgoing. He matched you with your world. You have exactly what you need to fulfill your destiny.

I have a friend who has a very strong personality. He's very kind and talented, but he's Type A, straight to the point, aggressive, a "get it done" guy. One day he and his wife were having a disagreement, debating something. She finally said, "Why can't you be more like Joel?" He responded, "Excuse me, but I think I'm supposed to be like Jesus." She said, "That's fine, but why don't you start with Joel?" We can always grow and improve, but you can't fight who God made you to be. Don't go your whole life wishing you were someone different, wishing you had a better personality, wishing you were more talented, wishing you were like your neighbor, when in fact you're exactly who you're supposed to be. What you don't realize is that half the time, your neighbor is wishing they could be you. They see all the good things about you, but do you? What would happen if you started loving yourself, accepting your gifts, not beating yourself up for mistakes,

Don't go your whole life wishing you were someone different, wishing you had a better personality, wishing you were more talented, wishing you were like your neighbor, when in fact you're exactly who you're supposed to be.

not down on yourself because of weaknesses? Stay positive toward yourself.

Most of us wouldn't criticize other people out loud. You wouldn't go up to a coworker and say, "You not looking so good today. Those clothes don't do anything for you." You may think it, but you wouldn't say it. So why are you criticizing yourself? When you criticize you, you're criticizing God's creation. You might as well look up and say, "God, You didn't do a good job on me." He doesn't make mistakes. Don't say another negative word about yourself. Don't say, "I'm so undisciplined. I can't do anything right. I don't have a good personality. I'll never lose this weight. I'll never break this addiction." Zip that up. Quit being against yourself. You don't need another enemy. Be as good to yourself as you are to others. Be kind to yourself, be merciful to yourself, be loving to yourself. When you get up in the morning and look in the mirror, instead of saying, "I'm getting so old. Look at all these wrinkles. It's all downhill from here," try a different approach. "I'm made in the image of God. I'm a masterpiece. I have royal blood flowing through my veins." Every time you do that, God is pouring strength, peace, and joy back into you.

Acknowledge the Good

A friend of mine is a pastor of a church in another state. For years, he would call me every Sunday after our service and tell me how good my message was. He's very encouraging. He would go on and on, one compliment after another. "That illustration was so effective, and this part is going to help so many people." Several years later, he came with me to an interview I was doing. It was a live, hour-long national program, a really big deal. I hadn't done many interviews like this before and I was nervous. When I finished and we got in the car, the first thing I said was, "I did really well. I said exactly what I wanted to say. I don't think I could have done it any better." He told me later how that conversation changed his life. When he saw how positive I was toward myself, he realized what his problem was. He had never once told himself that he had done well. After his services, he'd always drive home discouraged, thinking about how he could have done it better, how he wasn't focused enough, how he could have explained something more clearly. In all those years of pastoring, he never left the church feeling good. He always thought about what he didn't do right. When he heard me say, "I did well," a stronghold was broken in his thinking. He was great at complimenting others, but he had never complimented himself. He'd trained himself to see his flaws, his stumbles, and to focus on when he didn't do his best.

The Scripture says, "Our faith is made effective when we acknowledge everything good." You can't go around acknowledging the negative, your weaknesses, the times you didn't measure up, how you should have been more disciplined. Your faith is not going to be effective. You need to retrain your mind to see the good, to focus on what you did right. You didn't get everything done at the office, but you got something done. You haven't totally broken the addiction, but you're better than you were last year. You didn't spend all the time you wanted with your children, but you got them ready for school, got them dressed, and cooked their dinner. If you're acknowledging the negative, you're not going to feel good about yourself. Start acknowledging all the good things you're doing. That's what's going to help you do better.

You need to retrain your mind to see the good, to focus on what you did right.

Being down on yourself not only keeps you from enjoying life, but it keeps you from rising higher.

Every time I walk off the platform after a service, under my breath I say, "Lord, thank You for helping me do great today." I know I don't do great every time, but in my mind I do great. One Sunday I walked off the platform and my children were in the back. The first thing I said was, "I nailed it." They started laughing. I don't mean this arrogantly, but I celebrate myself. I compliment myself. I acknowledge what God has enabled me to do. I recognize that it's His favor, His anointing, His blessing on my life. I have plenty of areas in which to improve, and I know there are other people who can do it much better, which is okay. I'm not running their race. I feel good about me. You have enough enemies in life, so don't be against yourself. You should be your biggest fan. Nobody should think better of you than you.

> *You should be your biggest fan. Nobody should think better of you than you.*

Sometimes we're taught that if we think something good about ourselves, it's not being humble and lowly. No, you have to recognize that the Creator of the universe breathed His life into you. He's entrusted you with gifts, talents, and abilities. He's crowned you with favor. Don't go through life thinking little of yourself, focused on your weaknesses, dwelling on your failures. Start acknowledging the good, step into your potential, and show off that talent. Don't be your enemy; be your asset. When you acknowledge the good, when you say, "Lord, thank You for helping me to shine. Thank You for my gifts. Thank You for taking me where I've never dreamed," then your faith is made effective. You're going to see new doors open and new opportunities. You may be good at complimenting others, but now you need to get good at complimenting yourself. You don't have to do it out loud, but in your mind you need to say, "That was good. I got to work on time. And I did excellently on that presentation. That was good. I helped my neighbor last night. That was good." Why don't you start giving yourself the credit that you give others? You told your friend that she looked good, but have you told yourself that you look good? You complimented your coworker, but have you complimented yourself?

Mistakes Do Not Disqualify You

"Joel, I would feel good about myself, but I've made so many mistakes. I should have been more disciplined." The mistakes didn't change your purpose. Don't let failures and times when you got off course cause you to be against yourself. Be as merciful to you as you are to others. You have to learn to forgive yourself. The accuser will bring condemnation and guilt, and he'll whisper, "You don't deserve it." He would love for you to feel unworthy, down on yourself. Carrying the burden of guilt will wear you down. Don't fall into that trap. The apostle Paul said to the Colossians, "God sees you as holy, blameless, and without fault." Don't say, "But that's not me. I have all kinds of faults." We all have past faults. We've all made mistakes, compromised, and failed. But when you asked God to forgive you, He cleared your record. He sees you without fault. That's all good, and that's a fact. But the real question is, Can you see yourself without fault? As long as you're beating yourself up and living condemned, the problem is that you are your enemy. God has already said you're blameless, without fault. Get in agreement with Him. Nothing you've done has stopped your destiny.

The real question is, Can you see yourself without fault?

Jesus knew that one day Peter would deny Him, yet He still chose Peter as His disciple. Why didn't He just pick someone else? He knew that Peter was going to fail. He knew that Peter was hot-tempered and used bad language, but God doesn't disqualify you because you have weaknesses. If He did, none of us would have a chance. After Jesus rose from the dead, an angel appeared to Mary Magdalene and two other women at the tomb and told them to go tell the disciples, and specifically Peter, that Jesus was alive. Based on his denial of Jesus, Peter could have lived defeated and condemned and thought, *What was wrong with me?* But he made the choice that we all have to make. Peter forgave himself. He had mercy on himself. He didn't live looking in the rearview mirror, thinking about how he had blown it. Peter soon went on to give the inaugural address when the church was birthed on the day of Pentecost, when three thousand people came to know the Lord.

All through the Scripture, God used people who made mistakes. Abraham had a baby out of wedlock. David took another man's wife and had the man killed. Jonah refused to go and preach repentance to the city of Nineveh and ran from God. What did God do to Jonah? He rescued him and sent him a second time to the city of Nineveh. God doesn't disqualify us. The mistake we make is that we disqualify ourselves.

All through the Scripture, God used people who made mistakes.

Something Awesome Is in Your Future

When Moses was on Mount Sinai, receiving the Ten Commandments, he left his brother, Aaron, in charge of the Israelites. He was gone so long that the people said to Aaron, "Make us gods who will go before us." Aaron knew they only worshipped Jehovah. He had spoken for Moses when he told Pharaoh to let the people go. He had seen the miracles that God did in Egypt to deliver them from slavery and had seen God part the Red Sea. But he told the people to bring their gold, which he melted down and made into a golden calf. The people declared this as their God and started partying, with all kinds of revelry. When Moses came down the mountain, he saw the people were out of control and dancing naked, worshipping that idol. Moses had been on the mountain having this holy moment in the presence of the glory of God, yet in forty days the people had already fallen away under Aaron's leadership. You would think God would be done with Aaron. "If you can't lead My people for a couple of weeks, if you're going to give in to temptation and compromise that easily, then good riddance." But God doesn't write us off. He chose Aaron to be the first high priest for the nation of Israel. I can hear God saying to an angel, "You see that guy down there who made the golden calf and did not restrain the people. He's going to be the one I choose to go into the Holy of Holies, the most sacred place of the temple."

Don't judge your life based on one mistake or one season where you gave in to temptation and compromised. That didn't stop your destiny. The only way it will hold you back is if you live guilty, condemned, feeling washed up. God has forgiven you, but you have to forgive yourself. He's given you His mercy, but you have to have mercy on yourself. "Joel, you don't know what I did." You probably weren't dancing naked in public last week. You probably weren't making a golden calf to worship. Why are you writing yourself off? You don't

Don't judge your life based on one mistake or one season where you gave in to temptation and compromised.

know where God is taking you. Who would ever have thought that Aaron would become the high priest and be in a position of honor and influence? God has something awesome that's still in your future.

But here's the question: Are you for you? Are you kind to yourself? Are you merciful to yourself? You may love God, but do you love yourself? You forgive others, but will you forgive yourself? You compliment your friends, but will you compliment yourself? How much further will you go if you stay positive toward yourself? Quit beating yourself up for past mistakes, quit dwelling on your flaws, and quit overanalyzing your weaknesses. You're not a finished product. God is still working on you. I believe and declare that this is a breakthrough day in your life. Strongholds are coming down. Guilt is leaving, and a poor self-image is going. You are holy, you are blameless, and you are without fault. Get ready. I believe that you're going to be happier than you've ever thought possible and become everything God created you to be. You're about to rise higher, overcome obstacles, accomplish dreams, and fulfill His plan for your life.

Are you for you? Are you kind to yourself? Are you merciful to yourself?

CHAPTER THREE

Choose to Be Happy

You are as happy as you want to be.

When we wake up in the morning, we get to choose how we're going to live that day. We can choose to live in faith, to be happy, and to expect favor, or we can choose to live discouraged, defeated, and focused on our problems. Happiness doesn't automatically happen. It's a choice we have to make each and every day. You can't wait to see what kind of day it's going to be; you have to decide what kind of day it's going to be. The first thing in the morning, you need to make up your mind and say, "I'm going to live this day happy. I'm going to see the good. I'm going to be grateful. I'm going to love my family. I'm going to enjoy this day."

If you don't decide how you're going to live, circumstances will decide for you. You'll see every problem and think it's not going to work out. You'll think, *I don't feel like going to work. The traffic is so bad. I never get any good breaks.* When you dwell on those thoughts, you may not realize it, but you're choosing to live discouraged, and you're choosing to have a lousy day. The Scripture says, "Joy comes in the morning." Every morning, God sends you a fresh supply of joy. You can dismiss it and think, *That's not for me. I have too much coming against me.* Or you can receive it and say, "Things may not be perfect in my life, but I know that God is on the throne. He's ordering my steps, and His plans for me are for good, so I'm going to enjoy this day."

This is what David did. He faced all kinds of opposition, armies trying to stop him, people slandering him. But in the middle of that, he said, "This is the day the Lord has made. I will rejoice and be glad in it." His circumstances said that he should be discouraged, afraid, and lonely. If he was reporting on the situation, he would have said, "This is the day the Lord has made, and I'm really discouraged. I have a lot of problems." That would have been the truth. But he wasn't reporting; he was making a declaration of faith. He was saying, "Despite the opposition, I will be happy. Despite people lying about me, I will be happy. Despite my family not believing in me, I'm going to live this day happy." If you're going to be happy, you have to be happy on purpose, because there will be people, betrayals, delays, and all kinds of situations that can cause you to live sour. You have to put your foot down and say, "That's it. I'm not letting other people steal my joy. I'm not letting what's not working out to cause me to be sour. I'm not letting this problem at work keep me from enjoying my life. I will rejoice, and I will be glad. I will live this day happy."

> *If you're going to be happy, you have to be happy on purpose, because there will be people, betrayals, delays, and all kinds of situations that can cause you to live sour.*

Your will is more powerful than how you feel. David didn't feel happy when he wrote this, but he declared, "I will rejoice." Don't wait to feel happy before you decide to be happy. You have to decide first, then the happiness will come. As with David, you may feel discouraged. You may have a good reason—things were unfair, you went through a loss, nothing looks promising in your future. The enemy would love for you to think that's the way it's always going to be, to just drag through the day sour and never get your hopes up. No, you have to kick your will into gear. "I will be happy. I will enjoy this day. I will focus on the goodness of God." Your will is going to override how you feel. A mark of maturity is when you can be happy even when things aren't going your way, because your joy is not based on your circumstances.

Your will is more powerful than how you feel.

"Well, Joel, when this sickness is over, I'll get my joy back. When I finish school, I'll be happy again. When the Texans win the Super Bowl, I'll be in a good mood. (You may be waiting a while.) When I get married, I'll be happy. If I wasn't married, I'd be happy." If you're putting off your happiness, there will always be some reason to not be happy. Why don't you make a decision that you're going to be happy today? Not when it works out, not when your boss changes, not when you lose twenty pounds, not when you get the promotion. "This is the day the Lord has made."

You Control Your Own Happiness

I've learned that if you don't get happy where you are, you probably won't get to where you want to be. "I can't stand this job. I don't like working at this place." Try a different approach. "God, I'm happy that

If you don't get happy where you are, you probably won't get to where you want to be.

I have a job. Help me to not let these people steal my joy." If you have a good attitude where you are, that's a seed that God will use to change things. But if you're sour at that job, and God gives you a better job, when someone does you wrong there, you'll be sour at that place, too. You have to get happy where you are. "I may not be in my dream house yet, but I'm happy in this apartment. I'm not married yet, but I'm happy being single. This health issue hasn't resolved yet, but, God, I'm going to be happy while You're changing things." You control your own happiness. It's not up to anyone else. You're as happy as you want to be.

You're as happy as you want to be.

I played basketball with a young man who was always in a good mood, so friendly and upbeat. One day after a game, I asked if he wanted to go get something to eat. He said, "No, I have to go to the clinic. I'm taking chemotherapy." He had been fighting cancer for three years, which was a surprise to me. I couldn't tell anything was wrong. I said, "I'm so sorry to hear that." He said, "Don't feel sorry for me. Life is good. I'm blessed. I have a beautiful wife and a new son. I'm grateful to be alive." He could have been depressed, sitting around in self-pity and thinking, *Why me? This is not fair.* Instead, he made the choice to be happy where he was. I asked him how he could have such a great attitude. He said, "When I wake up in the morning, I ask myself, 'Do you want to live depressed, or do you want to live happy?' I choose to live happy." I wonder how much more we would enjoy our lives if we would do as he did and start choosing to be happy. We can't get away from negative circumstances. I can't tell you that having faith will keep you from trouble, bad breaks, or people who do you wrong, but I can tell you that those things don't have to take your joy. You're in control of your happiness.

David says in Psalm 144, "Happy are the people whose God

is the Lord." Sometimes we look at our circumstances, and there's nothing to be happy about. When you're fighting cancer, going through a pandemic, or having trouble at work, there's nothing good about that. The reason we can be happy is that our God is on the throne. He controls the universe. He's our provider, our healer, our vindicator, and our way maker. We can be happy that the most powerful force in the universe is on our side. No person can stop Him. No bad break, no sickness, no addiction, not even all the forces of darkness can stop what God has ordained for you.

The reason we can be happy is that our God is on the throne.

It's significant that David started off by saying, "This is the day the Lord has made." He could have just said, "I'm going to be glad today. I'm going to rejoice." He was saying, "God, I recognize that You not only made this day, but You've allowed me to be alive. You chose me before I could choose You. You formed me in my mother's womb. I'm not going to waste this day living negative, focused on my problems, dwelling on my hurts. I'm going to live this day to the full." You and I are not here by accident. God could have chosen anyone to be alive today. There are billions of people who have lived and died, but God handpicked you to be here at this time. He woke you up this morning. He gave you strength to get out of bed. He's crowned you with favor. He put seeds of greatness in you. He calls you more than a conqueror, the head and not the tail. One way we can honor God is by living happy. He didn't create you to drag through the day, overcome by problems, discouraged by disappointments. No, this day is a gift from God. We should feel a responsibility to live it in faith, to be happy, joyful, and good-natured. Once this day is over, we can never get it back. We

One way we can honor God is by living happy.

don't have time to waste another minute being negative, discouraged, focused on what didn't work out, complaining over who did us wrong. Get your joy back.

Have a Song of Praise Every Morning

"Joel, I'd be happier, but I've been through hurts. People have done me wrong." I say this respectfully, but everyone's been hurt. "I've had disappointments, bad breaks, and loss." We all have. You can use that as an excuse and let it sour the rest of your life, or you can say, "Father, thank You for entrusting me with another day. I'm not going to take it for granted. I recognize this is a day that You have made. I'm going to choose to be happy. I'm going to choose to enjoy this day. I'm going to live it to the full." When you have that kind of attitude, God will give you beauty for ashes, and He'll make up for the wrongs.

A while ago, there were some birds right outside our bedroom window. At five o'clock in the morning, they started chirping so loudly that they woke me up. All the different sounds, the singing and melodies went on for over an hour. One bird would chirp loudly, there would be a pause, then another would answer. At times they all chirped together, and it sounded like a symphony. I would have enjoyed it, but it was five o'clock in the morning and I wanted to sleep. The next morning at five o'clock the same thing, again and again. One morning it was cold and raining with thunder and lightning. I thought there's no way those birds were going to be happy and singing. But at five o'clock, right on cue, there came the birds, louder than ever. I wanted to ask those birds, "Why are you so happy? Don't you know we're in tough times?

Haven't you read the news? There are problems in the world, the price of gas is high, the supply chain is messed up. How can you be singing? What if you don't get your worms tomorrow?"

It's interesting how God put something in those birds to start the day off singing. They're saying, in effect, "Life is good. We're happy. We're going to enjoy this day." What would happen if we would have that song of praise every morning? As with those birds, what if we were not moved by our circumstances, but we sing in the dark, when things aren't going our way? We sing in the storm, when circumstances are against us. We sing in the cold, when we don't feel like it. We could be discouraged and complaining, but instead we're making the choice that we're going to live this day happy.

What if we were not moved by our circumstances, but we sing in the dark, when things aren't going our way?

I like to imagine that the reason those birds are so happy is they haven't watched the news. They haven't read the papers. They're not on social media. Nobody has told them they're supposed to be worried, afraid, and upset. It's as though they believe that their Heavenly Father is in control. It's as though they've seen Him take care of them in the past, and they believe He'll take care of them in the future. If you're going to live happier, you may have to tune some things out. You can't take in the negative all the time and stay in faith. The Scripture says, "Think on things that are of a good report, things that are

If you're going to live happier, you may have to tune some things out. You can't take in the negative all the time and stay in faith.

positive and hopeful." Our thinking has a lot to do with our happiness.

Think Happy Thoughts

The apostle Paul went through a lot of bad breaks. In 2 Corinthians 11, he lists some of these difficulties. Five times he received thirty-nine lashes. Three times he was beaten with rods. Once he was stoned. Three times he'd been shipwrecked. He was bitten by a poisonous snake. He faced angry mobs, fought off bandits, survived flooded rivers. He'd gone without food and proper clothing and spent sleepless nights. Nobody had more come against them than Paul. After being in prison for two years on false charges, he was brought before King Agrippa for his trial. In Acts 26, when he stood up to give his defense, the first thing Paul said was, "King Agrippa, I think myself happy." You would think he would see himself as a victim, be bitter and angry, with a chip on his shoulder. But he shows us a secret of how to overcome all that. He said, "I think myself happy." He said, "I consider myself fortunate to stand before you even though my accusers want me to be put to death." You can think yourself depressed, you can think yourself into a bad mood, and you can think yourself a victim. Or you can do as Paul did and say, "Yes, I've had a lot of difficulties. I could be sour and live discouraged, but I'm going to think myself happy."

He shows us a secret of how to overcome all that. He said, "I think myself happy."

As long as you're thinking about your hurts, what you didn't get, how you were left out, you're going to be discouraged. Why don't you start thinking happy thoughts? Happy thoughts are, *I have a bright future. Something good is going to happen to me. My latter days will be better than my former days. No weapon formed against me shall prosper.* I'm not saying to deny the negative, but I'm saying to not dwell on it. Don't relive what didn't work out. Don't replay the loss, the disappointment, or the failure. You can't move forward if you're looking back. You can't enjoy today if you're focused on yesterday. You may have had disappointments, things that were not fair, but you need to do as Paul did and start thinking yourself happy.

You can't move forward if you're looking back. You can't enjoy today if you're focused on yesterday.

I get up every morning and tell Victoria, "Today is going to be a great day." You know what I'm doing? Thinking myself happy. I'm getting my mind going in the right direction. It's easy to get up and think yourself sad, think yourself into self-pity. *Why did I come down with this illness? Why am I still single when all my friends are married? These people at work are not treating me right. This is not fair.* You're thinking yourself defeated. You have to change what you're thinking and say, "Yes, I came down with this illness, but, Father, I want to thank You that You're restoring health to me, that I will live and not die, that my best days are still in front of me." You have to say, "Yes, these people at work are not treating me right, but I'm not a victim. I know I'm a victor. God, You are my vindicator. You said You would always cause me to triumph." Happy thoughts are, *God, I'm grateful to be alive. I'm excited about my future. I believe*

When you think happy thoughts, it not only lifts your spirit, but that attitude of faith is what allows God to do amazing things.

You're taking me from glory to glory, that I haven't seen or imagined the great things You have in store. When you think happy thoughts, it not only lifts your spirit, but that attitude of faith is what allows God to do amazing things.

After Paul gave this great speech to King Agrippa, he was sent back to prison. His prayer wasn't answered. You would think that now surely he would be discouraged, surely he'd be complaining. No, in prison in Rome he wrote, "Rejoice in the Lord always, and again I say, rejoice." He was telling us that even when it doesn't go your way, just keep thinking happy thoughts. Keep giving God praise, keep thanking God that He's working, and keep being grateful when you could be complaining. Keep thinking victory when you're seeing defeat. Happiness is not dependent on what's going on around you; it's dependent on what's going on inside you. What kind of thoughts are you thinking? *I'll never get well. I've had this too long.* You're thinking yourself discouraged. *I can't break this addiction. It's been in my family for years.* You're thinking yourself limited. *I can't be happy. I've been through a lot of loss, a lot of heartache.* That's not how your story ends.

But here's a key: You have to give yourself permission to be happy. Sometimes we've bought into the lie that we're not supposed to be happy. We've been through too much and have made too many mistakes. If we're happy, we think that other people may not understand. Can I tell you that you're supposed to be happy? God created you to enjoy your life, to laugh and smile. Happiness starts inside. Give God something to work with. If you want to live happier and healthier, every morning you need to say to yourself, "I'm happy. I'm grateful. I'm blessed." You can't receive happiness if

You have to give yourself permission to be happy.

you're thinking sadness. Joy is coming every morning. Some people have been bypassing it year after year because of their thoughts. You will live happier if you start thinking happier.

Be Glad-Hearted

The apostle Paul wrote to the Thessalonians: "Be happy in the faith, glad-hearted continually." He was telling us again to think happy thoughts. Be glad-hearted. He didn't say anything about our circumstances. Be happy whether people treat you good or not. Be happy if your plans work out or if they don't. Be happy if you don't have any disappointments or if you have many. He was saying to get in a habit of thinking happy thoughts. Don't let the negative circumstances talk you out of living happy.

Don't let the negative circumstances talk you out of living happy.

I was driving down the road the other day, and I was in a hurry to get to an appointment. There was a car in front of me going twenty miles an hour in a forty-five mile an hour zone. It was a one lane street, with no way to pass. It wasn't a school zone. The driver wasn't elderly. I couldn't understand why they wouldn't go the speed limit. At that point, I had to make up my mind that I was going to think happy thoughts, because the thoughts that were coming were not happy. My first thoughts were to blow the horn, call them a name, and yell, "Get out of my way!" I was about to think myself upset. But I did what I'm asking you to do. "God, I know You're in control. You're ordering my steps. Thank You that it's a good day, that I'm healthy, that I'm blessed, and that I have a bright future." I just switched over to happy thoughts. Not long after that, they turned. I honked my horn and went on. Just kidding—I didn't honk.

In the Scripture, the prophet Habakkuk put it this way: "Though the fig tree does not bud and there are no grapes on the vines, though the olive crop fails and the fields produce no food." Everything was going wrong for Habakkuk. Business was down, his crops weren't producing, and his income was limited. If he would have stopped there, he would have been depressed and discouraged, dragging through the day. But he went on to say, "Yet will I rejoice in the Lord. I will joy in the God of my salvation." He was saying, "Even when I'm not seeing increase, even when things aren't going my way, even when slow drivers delay me, and even when the medical report hasn't improved, I'm not going to fall apart. I'm still going to think happy thoughts. I'm still going to thank God that I'm alive, that I have purpose, that good things are in store." Are you thinking yourself sad, thinking yourself discouraged, thinking yourself a victim? Do you realize how much of your joy and creativity that takes? It's time to start thinking happy thoughts.

Are you thinking yourself sad, thinking yourself discouraged, thinking yourself a victim?

I know a lady who is very joyful and always has a smile. Every time I'm around her, she's so good-natured and fun. She's had difficulties in her life. It hasn't been easy, but she's learned this secret to think happy thoughts. One day she was at a store and went up to the counter to purchase something. The man at the register asked how she was doing. She said with a big smile, very enthusiastically, "I'm blessed, and just grateful to be alive!" He looked at her and said, "Do you go to Lakewood?" She replied, "I do." He said, "I should have known it. Everyone who comes in here who's like you goes to Lakewood." I believe that believers should be the happiest people on earth. There should be a difference between us and people who don't honor God. When you go to work, everyone may be complaining, discouraged, talking defeat, but don't fall into that trap. Stay full of joy, keep a smile on your face, keep thinking happy thoughts. This world needs more happy people. We need more joy in the world. There's so much sadness, gloom, and despair. If we're not careful, we'll let what's happening around us get in us. That's why every morning you have to choose to be happy and say, "It's not about how I feel. I will rejoice. I will enjoy this day. I will be happy."

> *Believers should be the happiest people on earth.*

See Every Day as Your Best Day

When you think about the best day of your life, what day would it be? Perhaps it's the day you were married, the day your child was born, the day you found out you were cancer-free, or the day you moved into your new house. Those are all great days that we look back on with fond memories. But do you know what I believe the best day of your life is? Today. God has given you another day to be alive, another day to enjoy your family, another day to see the sunrise, another day of possibilities, to pursue your dreams and to go after your goals. Sometimes we let the pressures of life—the traffic, what somebody said, a challenge at

> *There's no such thing as an ordinary day. Every day is a gift from God.*

work—to keep us from enjoying the day. We think it's just another ordinary day, but there's no such thing as an ordinary day. Every day is a gift from God.

The Scripture says, "Our life is like a vapor. We're here for a minute and then we're gone." A hundred years from now, our time on this earth will all be finished. If we really understood how valuable each day is, we would live it happier. It's easy to take every day for granted, to just get up, go through the motions, deal with the challenges, and the day is gone. But if you have a new perspective and start seeing every day as your best day, you won't let the little things upset you. You'll take time to enjoy the people whom God has given you to love. You'll stop by and say hello to the neighbor who's lonely. You'll think more happy thoughts. You'll live with more gratitude. You'll make the most of each day.

> *You may have some difficulties, things you could be sour about, things that can take your joy, but if you keep it in the right perspective, recognizing that this day is a gift from God, that really it's the best day of your life, then it's much easier to live it happy, to not be sidetracked by all the worries, by what didn't work out, by who cut you off in traffic.*

A pastor friend of mine went to visit a thirty-five-year-old mother in the hospital. She had cancer and wasn't supposed to have lived through the previous night. He walked in, took her hand, told her that he loved her and that he was praying for her. Despite being so frail and having lost her hair, she smiled ever so warmly and said in a faint voice, "Pastor, this is the best day of my life." He was puzzled by what she meant, thinking that it didn't seem like a very good day for her at all. Then she added, "You see,

I didn't know if I was going to wake up this morning. Now God has blessed me with another day to see my children, another day to spend with my family." She went on to say, "If I make it through this day, tonight I'm going to look out the window and look at the stars. I'm going to enjoy the moonlight."

My prayer is that God would give us the same spirit to embrace even the most difficult days of our life with joy and gratitude as she did, that we always focus on the good and never take life for granted, that we get up each morning and think about all the things for which we can be grateful. You may have some difficulties, things you could be sour about, things that can take your joy, but if you keep it in the right perspective, recognizing that this day is a gift from God, that really it's the best day of your life, then it's much easier to live it happy, to not be sidetracked by all the worries, by what didn't work out, by who cut you off in traffic.

When the apostle Paul came to the end of his life, he said, "I want to finish my course with joy." We're all going to go to be with the Lord at some point. I don't want to go discouraged, feeling like a victim, and saying, "Look what I've been through. Why did this happen?" Let's go full of joy, seeing each day as the best day, getting up each morning and choosing to be happy. Let's say with David, "It's not about how I feel. I will rejoice. I will be glad." As Paul did, let's get in the habit of thinking happy thoughts. If you do this, I believe and declare that you're going to live happier, you're going to enjoy your life more. Forces that have held you back are being broken right now. God is about to release you into new levels of favor, freedom, and fulfilment. You will finish your course with joy.

CHAPTER FOUR

Let Go of Control

Hold tightly to your dreams, but hold loosely to how God is going to do it.

God puts promises and dreams in all our hearts. We know we're going to get well, we know our business is going to succeed, we know we're going to meet the right person. But God doesn't tell us how or when it's going to happen. Too often if it's not happening the way we thought or on our timetable, we get frustrated. "God, when is this going to turn around? When is my health going to improve? Why isn't this situation at work getting better?" We try to put God in a box and tell Him how to do it, when it should happen, and who to use. If it's not working out the way we think, we can get discouraged.

We try to put God in a box and tell Him how to do it, when it should happen, and who to use.

Once you pray, once you believe, you have to leave how God answers that prayer and when He does it up to Him. If you put a time frame on it and a method of how it's going to happen, you're going to be frustrated because God's ways are not our ways. He's working when we can't see it. Sometimes it's taking longer than we think because He has something better in store. One of the best things I've learned is to trust God's timing and trust His ways. What God promised will come to pass. But it may not happen the way you think, and it may not be when you had planned. If you're trying to control the outcome and control the time frame, you're going to live worried. You have to release control. You have to release having to have it happen your way.

God already has what's upsetting you figured out. He knows the end from the beginning. But here's the key: He doesn't give you the details. If you knew how everything was going to work out, it wouldn't take faith. If He told you, "Three months from now a big door is going to open. It may look as though you're going backward, but there's a shortcut that's going to put you ahead," you would relax and say, "Okay, it's all going to work out." Why don't you do that now? God has it all planned out. He's doing things you can't see. There are good breaks coming. The healing, the favor, and the right people are already on your schedule. If you release control of what is troubling you, you can enjoy your life while you're waiting for things to change. What's upsetting you? What's keeping you awake at night? God is saying, "Release it to Me. I'm in control. I'm ordering your steps. I'm working behind the scenes. It may not be good yet, but I'm going to turn it for your good."

> *What's upsetting you? What's keeping you awake at night?*

Enter into Rest

The Scripture says, "Those who have believed enter into rest." Once you've believed, you don't have to figure everything out. If you don't see anything changing, you'll be tempted to worry, but stay at rest. When you're at rest, you're showing God that you trust Him. Maybe you're believing for your health to improve, but the medical report is not getting better. You thought it would have happened by now. You could be worried and complaining, but instead you're thanking God, you're declaring His promises, you're being your best each day. When you're at rest, you're in faith. That's what allows God to work. But if you're upset over what's not changing, worried about your finances, and can't sleep because your child is off course, that's a sign that you've stopped believing. You need to enter into rest. Come back to a place of peace. You can't trust God and be worried at the same time. When you're at rest, you know that God is in control, you know that all things are going to work for your good, and you know that what He started, He's going to finish. When you're at rest, you're not stressed out, and you feel restored and revitalized.

You can't trust God and be worried at the same time.

"Joel, I'm worried about my finances. I'm upset about the medical report. When is this recession going to be over?" None of it is a surprise to God. He hasn't brought you this far to leave you. Release the worry, release the frustration, release having to know all the details. There will always be situations that we don't understand, problems that look too big, obstacles that seem permanent. Those are tests. Will you go through life worried, wondering if it's going to work out, discouraged because it's taking so long, or will you enter into rest? Will you believe that God is in control and that He will get you to where you're supposed to be?

My sister Lisa and her husband, Kevin, tried to have a baby for many years with no success. Lisa went through all of the fertility treatments, had a couple of surgeries, but still couldn't conceive.

Finally, the doctors told her that she wouldn't be able to have a baby. Lisa kept praying and believing, year after year, knowing that God has the final say. But at one point she realized she was consumed with having that baby. That was her main focus. Sometimes we want something so badly, it can get out of balance. We're not going to be happy unless God does it our way. You have to put those desires on the altar and give them to God. Don't release the dream, don't give up on the promise, but release control of how God is going to bring it to pass. He may not do it in a traditional way, in the way you were expecting. Anything that you have to have in order to be happy, the enemy can use against you. But when you can say, "God, this is what I want, but if it doesn't work out my way, I'm still going to be happy. I'm still going to give You praise," that takes away the power of the enemy. Hold tightly to your dreams, but hold loosely to how God is going to do it.

Anything that you have to have in order to be happy, the enemy can use against you.

Hold tightly to your dreams, but hold loosely to how God is going to do it.

A few months after Lisa released control, she received a phone call from a friend of ours in another state who has a home for teenage girls. One of the young ladies was about to give birth to twins, and she asked Lisa and Kevin if they would be interested in adopting them. They didn't have to think twice. They knew that was an answered prayer. A couple of months later, they were at the hospital when the babies were born. Today, they are beautiful young ladies in their twenties. God knows how to bring promises to pass, but you have to stay open to how it's going to happen. If you're set on having it one way, you can be frustrated. God does things out of the ordinary, in unusual ways. He may not bring your dream to pass in a traditional way. It seemed as though Lisa was falling behind, but with that one phone call she had not one but two babies. She didn't have to get pregnant and carry the baby for nine months. God did it an unusual way, and in a way that far surpassed any dream Lisa could have imagined.

Are you upset about something that's actually the hand of God at work? It hasn't happened yet because God is going to do something better than you think. The delay, the disappointment, or the setback is not working against you; it's working for you. Release control of how it's going to happen. God is about to do unusual things, out of the ordinary, unprecedented. You're not falling behind. You're about to receive a phone call, a good break, a promotion, your health suddenly turns around.

Are you upset about something that's actually the hand of God at work?

Your Set Time Is Coming

I've learned that God doesn't always take us down a straight path. There will be detours, delays, curves, and times when you feel as though you're going the wrong way. "God, I'm believing to go this direction, for promotion, healing, freedom, but I'm going the other direction. I'm in a downturn. I'm seeing just the opposite." Don't get set on the method. The way you think it's going to happen may not be the way God's going to do it. What you can't see is that on the path that's going the wrong way is a turn that leads to a shortcut that will catapult you ahead. Lisa was believing for one child and came out with two. That's the way our God is. Where

He's leading you is going to be better than you've imagined. The reason it's taking longer is because it's going to be bigger than you thought, more rewarding, more fulfilling. Doors aren't opening yet? You don't know what God is up to. You can't see what He's doing behind the scenes. People may be against you, the trouble hasn't turned around, and your family member is still off course. Don't be discouraged by what's not changing. Your time is coming.

The Scripture talks about how there is a set time for God to favor you, a set time to heal you, a set time to turn the problem around. If there's a right time, that means there's a wrong time. If it hasn't happened yet, it wasn't meant to be. Instead of fighting where you are, why don't you embrace where you are? "God, I know You're ordering my steps, and I'm right where I'm supposed to be. Thank You that my set times are coming." I can promise you this: God is not going to be one second late. He's not going to accidentally miss your set time.

If there's a right time, that means there's a wrong time. If it hasn't happened yet, it wasn't meant to be.

In July 2001, after a two-year battle to win the Houston City Council's vote for us to have the Compaq Center for our facility, we finally won. It was a miracle that we celebrated with the church, one of the greatest victories of our lives. The next day our family went out of town to take a few days off. We had no sooner arrived in our hotel room when I got a call telling me that a federal lawsuit had been filed against us that would keep us from moving into the Compaq Center. It stated that we were in violation of the deed restrictions. I was told that our case could be stuck in the legal system for ten years, with no guarantee that we would win. When Victoria heard the bad news, she sat down on the bed and asked, "Joel, what are you going to do?" I said, "I'm going down to the beach for a swim." She looked me in the eyes and said, "Aren't you worried?" I answered, "I can't change it, so I'm not going to worry about it. We did our part; now it's in God's hands. I'm going to stay at rest and trust God to fight this battle." It wasn't that I didn't battle worry and frustration over it in the coming days, but the lawsuit was suddenly dropped in January 2003, which felt like the Red Sea had parted. Our set time had come.

It's good to be passionate about our dreams, passionate about healing, freedom, and promotion. But don't be so consumed by it that you're not happy while you're waiting for God to bring it to pass. Don't put your happiness on hold until everything works out. This day is a gift. Enjoy your life while God is working. Enter into rest. Don't be uptight, stressed out, and asking, "When is it going to change?" You have to pass the test of being happy where you are before God gets you to where you want to be. If you can only be happy when the problem turns around, when you have the baby, when your business grows, that's going to delay what God is going to do. You have to put your foot down and say, "I am going to enjoy today and whatever it holds. The downturn, the challenges, and the bad breaks are not going to stop me. God is on His throne. I trust His timing, His ways. In the meantime, I'm going to live my life happy and believe in what is to come."

Trouble Is Transportation

Imagine if Joseph had not learned how to release control. In Genesis 37, God gave him a dream as a teenager that he would be in leadership and that people would bow down before him. What if he had a preconceived idea of how it was going to happen? What if he thought, *Surely, someone is going to come to my house, pick me out of a lineup with my brothers, show me favor, anoint me king, and I'll eventually step into leadership*, as God did for David several hundred years later? But God does things in unusual ways. He uses adversities, bad breaks, and disappointments to move us into our destiny. The trouble looks like a setback, but really trouble is transportation. God uses trouble to move you to where He wants you to be. We think God only uses favor, good breaks, and open doors. We know those are His blessings, and we thank Him when those happen, but I've learned that God uses closed doors just as much as open doors. He uses people who are against us just as much as people who are for us. He uses rejection, betrayals, and delays to position us for promotion. We can't see it at the time, it's uncomfortable, and we don't like it, but it's the hand of God ordering our steps.

> *God uses trouble to move you to where He wants you to be.*

Joseph had this dream. He knew God's favor was on him. What happened? He was betrayed by his brothers, thrown into a pit, sold into slavery in Egypt, falsely accused of a crime, and put in prison. He had one bad break after another. But Joseph understood this principle. He never complained. He never got bitter. I'm sure there were many lonely nights, times where he felt forgotten and abandoned, but deep down he could hear that still small voice telling him, "I'm still in control. I have you in the palms of My hands. This is all a part of your destiny." If he had tried to control it, tried to make it happen his way, he would have lived frustrated, angry, and bitter. Every day he had to release the worry, release the frustration, release how he thought it would happen. Thirteen years later, he became the prime minister of Egypt. He saw that dream come to pass.

When you study Joseph's journey, you see twists and turns, delays, detours, and disappointments. Proverbs 20 says, "Since the

Lord is directing your steps, why try to understand everything that happens along the way?" Are you frustrated because you don't understand something that's happened to you, upset over a bad break, worried because of a delay? How do you know it's not the hand of God leading you to your throne? How do you know that you're not just like Joseph? How do you know that you're not right on course, on schedule to see what God promised you? It may not happen like you think. God uses difficulties to position us for our destiny. What you're upset about is a necessary step. The closed door or the delay is instrumental in you reaching your purpose. Don't try to understand everything that happens along the way. God works in mysterious ways. If you're trying to figure everything out, you're going to get confused. There are things you're not supposed to understand. That's what faith is all about.

How do you know it's not the hand of God leading you to your throne?

If an adversity were going to stop your destiny, God wouldn't have allowed it. If a disappointment was going to keep you from your purpose, it wouldn't have happened. God is seeing what you're made of. This is your chance to say, as Joseph did, "God, I trust You even when I don't understand. I'm going to keep being my best even when it's not fair. I'm going to keep giving You praise when I could be complaining. I'm going to keep moving forward when I feel as though I'm going backward."

Stop Resisting and Start Resting

In Luke 22, Jesus was about to be crucified. He was on the Mount of Olives praying when Judas came up with a group of soldiers and kissed Him. That's how they knew whom to arrest. When they went to take Jesus, Peter pulled out his sword and cut off one of the ears of a servant of the high priest. Peter was ready to fight. He wasn't about to let this go down without opposition. The other disciples said, "Lord, should we fight? We brought our swords." Jesus answered, "Don't resist anymore." He was saying, "I understand how you feel. But this is all a part of My plan. This betrayal, the soldiers arresting Me, My being put on trial and being crucified—this is all leading to My destiny. It is all a part of My bringing salvation to the world."

It looked as though the enemy was in control, that the soldiers were getting the upper hand by taking Jesus away. They didn't realize they were taking Him into His destiny. When we face hardships, bad breaks, and disappointments, it seems as though the enemy is in control. That's when we want to fight and resist. That's when we get upset and live worried. But God is saying, "Don't resist anymore. Don't fight it. Don't live bitter. Don't try to get even. Trust Me. I'm in control. I'm still directing your steps." Yes, we have to resist sickness and resist addictions, but you shouldn't fight everything that comes your way. You shouldn't live upset and let it keep you awake at night. The enemy didn't get the upper hand; he didn't somehow get control of your life. God is still on the throne. The betrayal was unfair, but God didn't stop it because it's leading you to your destiny. You didn't like the disappointment. It looks as though the enemy is prevailing, as though the opposition is holding you back, but you don't know what God is up to. What you can't see is that on the other side of that crucifixion, so to speak, is a resurrection. On the other side of the betrayal, the sickness, or the disappointment is a new level of your destiny. Stop resisting and start resting.

Sometimes we're trying to play God. We try to straighten everybody out, vindicate ourself, fix the situation at work. Why don't

Sometimes we're trying to play God.

you release control? God doesn't need your help. He's not looking for some advice, hoping you'll stop those betrayals and keep those bad breaks from happening. No, don't resist anymore. Let Him be God. You don't have to fight everything that comes your way. You can't reach your destiny without a Judas kiss. Don't fight Judas; kiss him back and move on. You can't become who you were created to be without a Saul being jealous, as with David. You can't reach your throne as Joseph did without a Potiphar's wife falsely accusing you. Without a King Nebuchadnezzar throwing you into a fiery furnace as happened to the three Hebrew teenagers, you won't be honored and promoted. Without a Pharaoh trying to hold you captive, as the Israelites were, you won't reach your promised land. The good news is that the opposition is not in control. They become instruments in the hands of the Most High God. He is ordering your steps, and nothing happens without His permission.

You can't reach your destiny without a Judas kiss. Don't fight Judas; kiss him back and move on.

Let the Winds Blow You

In 1959, my father was successfully pastoring a church. They had just built a new auditorium, and he was on the state board for his denomination. Life was good. It looked as though he had a bright future there. But when my sister Lisa was born with something like cerebral palsy, my father went to a downtown hotel to be alone for a few days. He read the Bible as though it was the first time he had ever read it. He saw how God is a healer, and how He wants us to live a blessed, victorious life. He came back and started sharing his new message of faith and victory with his congregation. Much to his surprise, some of the church members didn't like it. It didn't fit into their tradition, and some of them said he needed to leave. He was so disappointed. He had spent years pouring his heart and soul into those people. My father could have fought it, made a big fuss, showed them he was right and they were wrong, but instead he didn't resist. He recognized that closed door was the hand of God, and he resigned from that church feeling rejected and betrayed. Then, he and my mother went out and started Lakewood in an abandoned feedstore with ninety people. Critics said it would never last, but over sixty years later we are still going strong.

God knew my father couldn't reach his destiny staying in that limited environment. Sometimes the best thing you can do is break away from negative people and put yourself in a healthy, positive, faith-filled environment. The people who were against him weren't bad people; they thought they were doing the right thing. But they became instruments in the hands of God to push my father into his highest potential. You have to be mature enough to know when to resist and when not to resist. You're not supposed to fight every battle. God uses betrayals, closed doors, and disappointments to move you into your purpose. What if my father had been bitter, stubborn, and not willing to move on? "God, I know You want me to pastor here." He could have missed his destiny. Don't try to control how your life is going to unfold and resist the unknown; release control and rest. Be open to what God is going to do.

> *You have to be mature enough to know when to resist and when not to resist.*

In Acts 27, Paul was a prisoner on a ship sailing toward Rome.

An angel appeared to him and said he was going to stand trial before Caesar. On the journey, they encountered a huge storm with hurricane-force winds. For fourteen days they didn't see the sun or the stars. They tried their best to steer the ship, to keep some kind of control, but the winds were too much. Instead of fighting it, trying to force where they wanted the ship to go, the Scripture says, "They took down the sails and let the ship go with the winds." When you've done everything you can, when you've prayed, you've believed, and you've stood in faith, there comes a time where you have to do as they did. Quit fighting it. Quit trying to force it to work out. Quit losing sleep and release control. God will not take you someplace where He won't sustain you.

How do you release control? Quit worrying about it, quit losing sleep, quit trying to make it happen your way, and say, "God, I trust You. I know You're in control of these winds. They can blow me forward, backward, left, or right, but there's one thing I'm certain of: Where You take me is exactly where I'm supposed to be." That's what my father did. He let those winds blow him to Lakewood. If you stay in faith, God will shift the winds that were meant to stop you, and instead of blowing you backward, those winds will blow you forward. That's what the Scripture says: "What is meant for harm God will turn to your advantage." Are you resisting or are you resting? Are you trying to control everything, trying to force it, and living upset because it's not happening your way? Why don't you take down the sails and trust what God is doing? You may not understand it now, it may

If you stay in faith, God will shift the winds that were meant to stop you, and instead of blowing you backward, those winds will blow you forward.

not make sense yet, but one day you'll see it was a necessary step to reach your destiny. It looked like a setback, but really it was a setup.

What You Can't See

I talked with a young lady whose life was going great until she was diagnosed with tuberculosis. She was out of work for so long that she lost her job. She couldn't afford her apartment, so a friend gave her a place to stay. She ended up getting a job with a major airline. She was so excited to finally be getting back on her feet, then the pandemic hit. When the airline cut her work back to only a few hours a week, she had to get an additional job working for a security company. One night, her truck was stolen at work. It was one bad break after another. She got a rental car, and it had SiriusXM radio. She said she was so discouraged that she needed to laugh, so she started flipping through the channels searching for a comedian. She came across our station, channel 128, and thought I sounded like a comedian. She started listening and found out that I wasn't, but she couldn't turn it off. Hope began to fill her heart with a fresh vision, dreams started coming back to life, and she ended up giving her life to Christ.

Recently, the security company offered her the opportunity to transfer to Hawaii and take a management position. She'd always dreamed of living there. Because she works for the airline, she can travel back and forth at no charge. She said, "I look back now at all the things that happened to me, and I realize it was all working for my good. If my truck hadn't been stolen, I wouldn't have come to know the Lord. If I didn't work for the airline, I wouldn't have the free flights. If they hadn't cut my hours back, I wouldn't have taken this job, and I wouldn't have had this new opportunity to move to Hawaii." She couldn't see it at the time, but the winds of that storm were blowing her to where God wanted her to be.

The difficulty and troubles that you're facing are not going to stop you. The trouble is transportation. Don't fight everything, live worried, and ask, "Why did this happen?" God knows what He's doing. He has you in the palms of His hands. He may not do it the way you had planned, but where He's taking you is better than you've imagined.

Psalm 55 says, "Cast your burdens on the Lord, release the weight of them, and He will sustain you." How many weights are you carrying around? Perhaps it's the weight of worry, the weight of what you don't understand, or the weight of how you're going to make it through a tough season. Those weights are not only wearing you down emotionally and mentally, but even physically. There's something you have to do. God is not going to take the burden away. You have to release the worry, release the frustration, release having to figure it out. Come back to a place of peace. The right attitude is: *God, my life is in Your hands. I commit my dreams, my family, my finances, and my health to You. I'm not going to fight everything I don't like. I'm not going to live upset when it doesn't go my way. I know You're working all things for my good. I trust Your timing. I trust Your ways.* When you have believed, you enter into rest. I'm asking you to stop resisting and start resting. If you release control, I believe and declare that the weights that have burdened you down are lifting off you right now. God is about to shift the winds of that storm. Instead of blowing you backward, it's going to blow you forward. Promotion is coming, healing is coming, freedom is coming, the fullness of your destiny.

How many weights are you carrying around?

CHAPTER FIVE

Unclutter Your Mind

You won't give birth to your dreams if your mind is a noisy place.

It's easy to go around worried about our future, stressed over our finances, frustrated with our boss. We're tempted to live feeling guilty about past mistakes, bitter over what didn't work out, upset about the person who did us wrong. We wonder why we can't sleep at night, why we don't enjoy our life, why we're not passionate about our dreams. It's because our mind is cluttered. You can't stop negative things from coming, but you can keep them from staying. You don't have to hold on to them. When you make mistakes, guilt will come, and condemnation will tell you how you don't measure up. You can hold on to it and go around being down on yourself. Or you can let it go and say, "Father, thank You that I am forgiven, that I'm redeemed. The past is over. This is a new day."

When something doesn't work out and you get disappointed, you can hold on to it and live discouraged. Or you can let it go and say, "God, I know You have something better. I know that Your plans for me are for good. I know that You're directing my steps." When the medical report is not good, when the contract doesn't go through, when you're facing a legal situation, you can live worried, stressed out, and be thinking, *What am I going to do?* Or you can let it go and say, "God, I know that You are fighting my battles. I know that what was meant for my harm, You're turning to my advantage. I don't see a way, but I know that You have a way." You can clear out the clutter. You can get rid of negative thoughts that are stealing your peace, taking your joy, and draining your energy. That's why the Scripture tells us to guard our minds. You have to be proactive if you're going to keep your mind in peace, because all through the day there's clutter. There's noise, there's drama, stress, worry, guilt, and jealousy. They may come, but you don't have to hold on to them.

You can get rid of negative thoughts that are stealing your peace, taking your joy, and draining your energy.

It's Time for an Intervention

I watched a documentary on hoarders, people who don't throw anything away. One lady lived by herself in a two-story house, but there was no way to get to the upstairs. The house was piled full of old newspapers, empty cereal boxes, and cans from food she had eaten thirty years ago. There was a small path so she could walk to the kitchen, to the bathroom, and to a little place to sleep, with big walls of trash on each side. You can imagine how it smelled and how unhealthy it was. It was so bad the authorities came to do an intervention. They knocked on the front door, but she couldn't open it. They had to go to a small side door and squeeze through it. At one point, one of the authorities picked up some of what looked like thousands of popsicle wrappers in the corner of a room and asked if they could get rid of them. She told him that those were from her children, that they meant something to her, and he should put them back. Her children were in their forties. It was obvious to everyone else that all she was doing was keeping trash, but she couldn't see it. She was so focused on holding on to everything from the past that she didn't realize how it was limiting her life and keeping her from living in the present and creating new memories with her loved ones.

How many of us are hoarders in our minds? We're not letting any negative thoughts go. There's so much clutter that we can't enjoy our life. We go to sleep at night but wake up tired in the morning because we couldn't rest. Our mind was working all night. God has you reading this because He wants to do an intervention. He wants to help you get rid of the worry, the hurts, the offenses, the frustration. Those things are limiting your life. What's interesting is that those authorities didn't make the lady throw things away. It was her choice. Eventually, she decided to do it. It wasn't easy. Everything in her mind said to hold on to the trash. That's all she had known for years. Living cluttered had become normal to her. She didn't think anything was wrong with having trash piled up in her house.

> *How many of us are hoarders in our minds?*

Sometimes we've been living worried for so many years that it's become normal to us. Living guilty is what we're used to. We've gone around feeling as though we don't measure up, we don't deserve to be blessed, and we've made too many mistakes. We've let those recordings play for so long that we've accepted them. Or maybe we grew up feeling less-than and living inferior. Thoughts have always

> *Sometimes we've been living worried for so many years that it's become normal to us.*

told us that we're not talented, we're not attractive, we don't have a good personality. We didn't know any better. We believed those lies for years. Now our mind is cluttered. The good news is, this is your day for an intervention. It's time to clear out the clutter. God is not going to force you to do it. This is a choice you have to make.

You need to say to those thoughts that are telling you that you're not up to par, "No, thanks. You're not welcome here. I am fearfully and wonderfully made. I have royal blood flowing through my veins. I am wearing a crown of favor." Clear out the negative. You have enough people in life against you; don't be against yourself. You were created in the image of the Almighty God who doesn't make any mistakes. He didn't make you faulty. He calls you a masterpiece, a prized possession. My challenge is, don't criticize what God has created. Don't say another negative word about yourself.

Don't criticize what God has created. Don't say another negative word about yourself.

A Prepared Table in the Presence of Your Enemies

The hoarder lady had a beautiful house but couldn't enjoy it. She couldn't go upstairs because of the trash. In the same way, if you don't clear out the clutter, it will keep you from going to new levels. Worry will keep you from rising higher. Being bitter will keep you from new opportunities. Living stressed will cause you to have health problems. Going around feeling guilty will keep you from pursuing your dreams. I'm asking you to unclutter your mind.

"Well, Joel, those people hurt me. They did me wrong. That's why I'm bitter. That's why I'm upset." That happened twenty-seven years ago. Why are you still holding on to it? Why are you still sour over the person who walked away, still bitter over how you were raised, still upset over the company that did you wrong? Don't be a hoarder. Don't let them poison your future. They hurt you once; don't let them continue to hurt you. Recognize that is cluttering your mind. That's limiting your vision. That's stopping the new things that God has in store for you. I'm not saying what they did wasn't hurtful. I'm not making any excuses for their behavior. But as long as you hold on to it, you're giving them your power. You're letting them control you.

You have only so much emotional energy each day. Do you know how much energy it takes to hold a grudge, to be bitter, to think about how you can pay somebody back? That's wasting valuable energy you need for your dreams, for your family, for your destiny. God said He would give you beauty for the ashes, but here's the key: You have to let go of the ashes before you can receive the beauty. You can't hold on to the hurts, live offended and bitter, and see the new things that God has in store for you. You have to clear out the clutter. That's what makes room for God to give you the beauty.

Do you know how much energy it takes to hold a grudge, to be bitter, to think about how you can pay somebody back?

The mistake we make is that we think we have to get even. We need to pay them back. That's not your job. If you turn it over to God, He'll be your vindicator. He'll bring justice into your life. He saw every wrong, every hurt, every person who took advantage of you. I've learned that God will vindicate you better than you can vindicate yourself. David says in Psalm 23, "God will prepare a table before you in the presence of your enemies." This means that when God brings you out, the people who did you wrong, the people who tried to hold you back, and the people who said you don't have what it takes will see you promoted, honored, and in a position of influence. God is not going to vindicate you in private. He's going to do it in public so your enemies see you blessed, favored, and successful.

When God brings you out, the people who did you wrong, the people who tried to hold you back, and the people who said you don't have what it takes will see you promoted, honored, and in a position of influence.

When my father went to be with the Lord and I stepped up to pastor the church, I was very insecure. I had never ministered before. One Sunday morning right after I had finished ministering, I was walking through the lobby and overheard two older ladies talking. One said, "He's not as good as his father." The other answered, "Yes, I don't think he's going to make it." That was the last thing I needed to hear. It was like my worst nightmare. I was already tempted to shrink back and think, *I can't do this. I don't have the training. Nobody's going to want to hear me.* But I felt something rise up in me so strongly. I thought, *Who are they to tell me what I can't do? They don't determine my destiny. They didn't breathe life into me. They didn't know me before I was formed in my mother's womb. They didn't call me, they didn't equip me, and they didn't anoint me. They don't have to be for me. I don't need their approval.*

I did what I'm asking you to do. I cleared out the clutter. Every time their voices came to my thoughts, I said, "No, thanks. I am well able. I am strong in the Lord. God being for me is more than the world being against me." Those two ladies still may not like me, but that's okay. When they turn on the television, they'll probably see me. When they flip through SiriusXM radio, they will probably hear me. What is that? God preparing a table in the presence of my enemies.

Be Still and Know

When we were trying to acquire the Compaq Center for our facility, a friend of mine was at a luncheon where a well-known business leader told the whole group of local business executives that it would be a cold day in Hell before Lakewood would ever get the building. He and some other high-powered people were very against us. He didn't know this person was my friend. All the odds were against us. We were up against a company that was much bigger and had more resources, but God made things happen that we could never have made happen, and we got the building. I can imagine that every time that businessman drives down the freeway now and sees the building with the big Lakewood sign, he must think it's a cold day in Hell. What was that? God honoring us in front of our enemies. I'm not gloating over it. I'm just saying that God knows how to vindicate you. It would be one thing if He did it in private, and we would be grateful for that, but He's going to do it in public. He's preparing the table in the presence of your enemies.

This means that when you have opposition, when you have trouble, when people come against you, God has a table there. The key is to not fight with the opposition, to not try to pay people back or prove your point, to not live upset, worried, or frustrated. No, take a seat at the table that God has prepared. If you stay at rest, God will go to work. But when you work, God will rest. As long as you're worried, trying to make things happen in your own strength, that will limit what God will do. God says in Psalm 46,

> *If you stay at rest, God will go to work. But when you work, God will rest.*

"Be still, and know that I am God." Clear out the worry, clear out the offense, clear out the negativity. Live from a place of peace, a place of rest, a place of faith. God has you in the palms of His hands. Nothing you're facing is a surprise to Him.

In 2 Chronicles 20, when the Israelites were facing a vast enemy army, He told them, "Stand still, and you will see the Lord deliver you." He wasn't just talking about physically; He meant to be still in their minds, in their attitudes. As they did, you may have plenty of good reasons for why you could be worried, upset, and not able to sleep at night, but when you're at peace, that's a position of power. When you're in peace, you're showing God that you trust Him. Anyone can stay in faith and have a good attitude when everything is going their way. The test comes when the medical report is not good, when a friend walks away, when the loan doesn't go through, when your child is off course. You could easily let all the clutter in. No, be still. That's the time to show God that you trust Him, not just with your words but with your actions.

> *When you're at peace, that's a position of power.*

Who Fights Your Battles?

The enemy's main target is our mind. Our mind is the control center of our life. He wants to get our mind cluttered, filled with doubts. *What if it doesn't work out? What if my health doesn't improve? What if I don't get that contract?* As long as our mind is cluttered, it keeps God from turning things around. God works where there's faith.

In 2 Chronicles 32, the king of Assyria invaded Judah with a huge army and laid siege to their large fortified cities, breaking through their walls and capturing the people. The city of Jerusalem was next in line, and word quickly spread through the city. No doubt the people were worried, panicked, and thinking, *What are we going to do? They're so much bigger than us.* King Hezekiah gathered the people in the city square and said, "Don't be afraid of this mighty army. For there is a power far greater on our side. He may have a great army, but they are just men. We have the Lord our God to fight our battle for us."

When you are facing a big enemy, you have to remind yourself that our God is bigger than any cancer, bigger than the people trying to stop you, bigger than the addiction, bigger than the financial problem. The way to stay in peace is to not talk about how big the enemy is, but talk about how big your God is. He flung stars into space, He spoke worlds into existence, He parted the Red Sea, He healed my mother of terminal cancer, and He gave us the Compaq Center. The good news is, He's breathing in your direction right now. He's pushing back forces of darkness. Don't let fear clutter your mind. Don't let doubt keep you from your miracle. Don't let what people say talk you out of your dream.

The way to stay in peace is to not talk about how big the enemy is, but talk about how big your God is.

The king of Assyria sent a letter to the Israelites, trying to intimidate King Hezekiah and all the people of Judah. It read: "We've captured all these cities along the way, overtaken all these people, and none of their gods saved them. What makes you think your God is going to save you?" The enemy will always try to defeat you in your thoughts first. *Joel, you can't get up in front of people. You don't have the training or the experience.* Thoughts will whisper, *You're not going to get well. Your grandmother died of the same thing. You'll never break that addiction. You'll never meet the right person.* Don't believe those lies. He wouldn't be telling you that if he didn't know it was already on the way.

Do as Hezekiah did and say, "This problem may be big, but I know a secret: My God is bigger. He's on the throne. He has the final say. What He started, He's going to finish." Had Hezekiah not been proactive to guard his mind and to speak victory to the people, they would have all panicked and lived stressed out, but instead they stayed in peace. After Hezekiah and the prophet Isaiah prayed, it says, "God sent an angel who destroyed the whole army, all the commanders and officials. The Assyrian king returned home in disgrace to his land." God knows how to vindicate you. He knows how to turn that problem around. One angel took care of the whole bunch. Stay in faith. When you're tempted to worry, turn it into worship. "Lord, thank You that You're fighting my battles. Thank You that no weapon that is formed against me will prosper. Thank You that the enemy will fall into the trap they themselves set for me."

When you're tempted to worry, turn it into worship.

Just Do Your Part

If you're going to keep the clutter out, you have to know what your job is and what God's job is. Sometimes we're frustrated because we're trying to do what only God can do. There are some things we can't fix. You can't make yourself get well, make somebody else do what's right, or make some doors open. Our part is to believe, our part is to stay in faith, and then let God do His part. Trust Him to work it out. Hezekiah could have thought, *God is on my side. I'm going to go attack that king's army and let him know who he's dealing with.* We wouldn't be reading about him if he had. I'm not saying to sit back and be passive, but there are some battles that you're not supposed to fight. Let God fight them for you. With the Compaq Center, it was a three-year battle. We did what we could, but we realized it was too big for us and said, "God, only You can make this happen. We're going to be still and know that You are God." As with Hezekiah, God stepped in and made things happen for us that we could never have made happen.

There are some battles that you're not supposed to fight. Let God fight them for you.

While you're waiting for God to change things, that's a test. It's easy to live worried, to stay focused on the problem, to think about why it's not going to work out. Clear out that clutter. The prophet Isaiah says, "You will keep him in perfect peace, whose mind is stayed on You." Our part is to keep our mind on Him. "Father, thank You that You're in control. Thank You that You are for me. Thank You that Your destiny for my life will come to pass." When we do our part, God will do His part. He'll not only keep you in peace, but He'll get you to where you're supposed to be.

In Daniel 3, three Hebrew teenagers were about to be thrown into a fiery furnace because they wouldn't bow down to the king's golden idol. The king threatened them one last time, but they said, "King, we're not going to bow down. We know our God will deliver us." They had this attitude of faith. But what they said next was the real key: "But even if He doesn't, we're still not going to bow down." That's a powerful position. When you can say, "I'm going to stay in peace if it works out my way, and I'm going to stay in peace if it doesn't work out my way," you take away all the power of the enemy. If you're only going to be happy if it happens the way you want, you're setting yourself up for disappointment. Why don't you take it one step further and say, "God, You know what's best for me. This is what I want, this is what I'm believing for, but even if it doesn't happen, I'm still going to stay in peace. I'm still going to be my best. I'm still going to have a song of praise. God, I trust You." That's what allows God to do amazing things.

If you're only going to be happy if it happens the way you want, you're setting yourself up for disappointment.

Live Out of a Quiet Place

There's a lot of noise these days, a lot of drama, things we can get pulled into. There's a lot of worry, offenses, doubt, and jealousy. That may be around us, but it doesn't have to get in us. Pay attention to what you're allowing into your spirit. Just because there's strife in your family or division in your workplace doesn't mean it has to get in you. Stay on the high road. Don't take the bait. At work, you could be frustrated with the office politics, with people who aren't treating you right. It's easy to let that sour your day, and you come home negative. No, clear out that clutter. Your time is too valuable to live it offended and upset. Life is flying by. We can never get this day back. Live it in peace, live it in faith.

Sometimes we're so hooked on drama, we're so used to being on edge, putting out one fire after another, worrying about situations, or fighting with a relative that we've forgotten what it's like to not have all this clutter and to be in peace. But God created us to live in peace. In the garden of Eden, before Adam and Eve ate the forbidden fruit, there wasn't any traffic, any jealousy, any politics, any worry, or any backstabbing. It was peaceful, and they were joyful. Yes, things changed, and it's not like that now, but you can still live from a place of peace. You don't have to let what's outside get inside. Maybe you've gotten comfortable with the clutter. Like the hoarder lady, not only don't you realize that it smells, but it's blocking your vision, it's limiting your potential. Worry doesn't look good on you. Being offended, stressed, and jealous is not your style. Clear out the clutter, and you'll step into new levels.

Sometimes we're so hooked on drama, we're so used to being on edge, putting out one fire after another, worrying about situations, or fighting with a relative that we've forgotten what it's like to not have all this clutter and to be in peace.

I've read that a sheep won't give birth in a noisy place. When it starts to go into labor, it will leave the flock, get away from all the commotion, all the busyness, and find a quiet place. In that peaceful atmosphere, it will give birth. In a similar way, you won't give birth to your dreams if your mind is a noisy place. You won't give birth to the breakthrough you're believing for if your mind is worried and stressed. You won't give birth to your potential if your mind is full of hurts, regrets, and bitterness. Maybe you're wondering why God isn't doing anything. Perhaps He's waiting for you to find a quiet place. It may be noisy all around you, but in your mind you can be at peace. When you know that God is in control, when you know He's directing your steps,

You won't give birth to your dreams if your mind is a noisy place.

when you know nothing can stand against Him, then you can live out of a quiet place. An uncluttered mind is a powerful force.

This is what David says in Psalm 23: "God makes me to lie down in green pastures. He leads me by the still waters." You might think that as a king, David had an easy life, that everything went his way, that he, in effect, lived in the green pastures. It was just the opposite. His life was full of challenges, people trying to push him down, armies trying to defeat him, and even his own family didn't believe in him. Yet he said, "I lie down in green pastures by still waters." He wasn't just talking about physically; he was talking about in his mind. Despite all that came against him, He lived out of a place of peace. God is saying to you, "Come into the green pastures, come by the still waters." You don't have to carry all the clutter. It's time to clear out the worry, the offenses, the fear, the doubt. There are some new things God wants you to birth. Do you know where you're going to birth them? By the still waters. If you'll be still, you'll know that He is God. You'll see Him show out in your life. But it implies that if you don't get still, you'll miss the fullness of what He has in store.

It's time to clear out the worry, the offenses, the fear, the doubt. There are some new things God wants you to birth.

I wonder how much more you would enjoy life, how much longer and healthier you would live, if you choose to unclutter your mind. Living guilty is not your destiny. Going around being down on yourself or thinking your problems are too big is not who you were created to be. Empty out all the negative, and program your mind with what God says about you. If you do this, I believe and declare that you're not only going to enjoy your life more, but you're going to give birth to dreams, to favor, to breakthroughs, to healing. God is going to take you further than you've imagined.

CHAPTER SIX

Dealing with Difficult People

You can't control how everyone treats you, but you can control how you respond.

I thought about titling this chapter "Dealing with Friends, Family, and Coworkers." There's someone at work who has a way of getting on your nerves, or a friend who gets jealous and gives you the silent treatment, or a child who is really difficult. It might be a neighbor who's rude or a relative who's not for you and talks about you. How you handle difficult people will determine how high you will go. If you treat them the way they treat you, you'll get stuck. If they're disrespectful, and you're disrespectful back, that will keep you from going further.

How you handle difficult people will determine how high you will go.

The Scripture says, "You overcome evil with good." You never overcome disrespect with more disrespect. You never get ahead by doing to others the wrongs they did to you. That's a test of your character. God is seeing what He can trust you with. Will you be the bigger person and overlook the insult? Will you stay on the high

Will you stay on the high road and not get baited into conflict?

road and not get baited into conflict? You only have so much emotional energy each day. It's not an unlimited supply. It takes a lot of energy to get upset, to live offended, to think about what someone said about you, and to try to straighten them out. That's energy you need for your dreams, to pursue your goals, to enjoy your family. Don't spend it on things that don't matter.

You can't control how everyone treats you, but you can control how you respond. When someone is rude, you don't have to get upset. When they cut you off in traffic, that doesn't have to ruin your morning. When a coworker leaves you out, you can't control that, but you can stay in peace, knowing that God is fighting your battles. When you take the high road, you'll not only enjoy your life more, but you're showing God that He can trust you with more influence, with more favor. Don't go the next twenty years letting the same situations upset you, the same coworker get on your nerves, or the same grumpy relative steal your joy. They may not change, but here's the key: You can change. Sometimes we've trained ourselves to respond a certain way. "If they say this, I'm going to get upset. If they leave me out, I'm going to leave them out. If my crazy uncle makes fun of me, I'm going to tell him off." The problem is, you're letting them control you. If they perform a certain way, it's going to sour your day. Why don't you take the controls back?

Why don't you take the controls back?

Heap Coals on Their Heads

Jesus says, "Stop allowing yourself to get upset." Someone can't make you get upset; you have to give them permission to upset you. You have to make the choice: *I'm offended. I'm discouraged. I'm sour.* Some people know exactly what buttons they can push to get you bent out of shape. The next time they push those buttons, just smile and say, "Not this time. I'm staying in peace. I'm going to enjoy this day."

If someone is disrespectful, rude, and always finding fault, they have issues they haven't dealt with. They end up with bitterness, anger, and insecurity bottled up inside. Sometimes that poison will try to spill off on you. You have to stay on the offensive. "They may be rude, but I'm not taking the bait. I'm staying calm. I'm going to be respectful, despite how they treat me." Or, "My boss celebrates everyone except me. He gives others credit for my work, but I'm not going to live sour. I'm not working unto people. I'm working unto God." You may say, "Joel, if I always take the high road, people will take advantage of me. I'll look weak. I have to stand up for myself." But you never go wrong by taking the high road. You never lose out when you're kind, when you overlook an offense, when you choose to stay in peace.

The Scripture says, "When you're good to your enemies, it's like heaping coals of fire on their heads." You would think that if we treat our enemies the way they treated us, that would be good payback. "If they talk bad about me, I'm going to talk bad about them. If they leave me out, I'm going to leave them out. If she's rude to me, two can play at that game. I'll be rude to her." To let them have it feels good to our flesh, but you never come out ahead by doing to others the wrongs that they did to you. The real way you see favor and increase is when you bless your enemies. To "heap coals of fire on their heads" means to provide your enemy with fire for their household when they've let their coals die out overnight. When

> *You never come out ahead by doing to others the wrongs that they did to you.*

you're good to those who are not good to you, not only will you rise higher, but God will deal with those who are not treating you right. He knows how to use those coals of fire, how to take your kindness and put pressure on them and make them think differently about you.

Spread Your Wings and Rise Higher

In the Scripture, the believer is referred to as an eagle several times. The prophet Isaiah says, "You will mount up with wings like eagles." It's significant that God chose an eagle. An eagle can fly at altitudes of ten thousand feet or more and can soar in the air for hours riding on natural wind currents and thermal updrafts. I read that crows are natural pests to the eagle. Although the eagle is bigger and stronger, the crow is more agile. It can turn quicker, maneuver faster. Sometimes to annoy the eagle, the crow will follow right behind the eagle, just pestering it, trying to cause it trouble. The eagle could turn around and try to fight, thinking, *I'm bigger than this crow. I'm going to show him who I am.* Instead, when the eagle is tired of dealing with the crow, it doesn't try to outmaneuver the crow, moving left and right. It simply starts flying higher and higher. The crow can't go where the eagle can go. It rarely flies higher than a thousand feet, and eventually it will fall away.

> *The crow can't go where the eagle can go.*

In life, there will always be some crows. You may work with crows, you may have neighbors who are crows, and you may be sitting by a crow right now. (Just laugh. They won't know it.) There will always be people who can get on your nerves. They feel as though it's their calling in life to annoy you, irritate you, and push your buttons. That will continue to happen as long as you stay down at their level. You'll get upset, be baited into conflict, and live offended. You'll walk around with knots in your stomach from the stress that can lead to digestive problems and ulcers. You have to realize you're an eagle. The way you get rid of crows is not engaging with them, but by going up higher. Don't pay attention to what they're saying, quit reading the negative comments on social media, and don't let those offenses get down in your spirit. If you let that in, you'll get drawn into conflict.

You're an eagle. You're not supposed to be fighting with crows. You're not supposed to be upset with some chickens that are pecking around, trying to get you to deal with things that don't matter. Quit being frustrated by the turkeys, the people who don't understand you, the people who make a lot of noise trying to steal your peace. Those are distractions, trying to get you off course, wasting time and energy that you need for pursuing your goals.

You can't stop the crows from crowing. You can't stop the chickens from pecking. You can't stop the grouchy neighbor or the critical coworker from being rude, offensive, or disrespectful. But you can spread your wings and rise higher. You don't have to get engaged in petty things that don't matter. You were created to soar, designed to do big things, to leave your mark, to be a history maker. Don't waste your valuable time dealing with crows. There will always be people who don't understand you, people who are not for you, who try to hinder your calling. Yes, they'll say hurtful things, try to make you look bad, and put you at a disadvantage. Our human nature says to get in there and fight, straighten them out, show them what we're made of. Don't take that bait. That's a distraction.

You were created to soar, designed to do big things, to leave your mark, to be a history maker.

They don't control your destiny. They didn't breathe life into you. They didn't choose you before you were formed in your mother's womb. What they say cannot stop your purpose. Don't give it the time of day. Ignore it and move forward. Do you know what will happen? The crows will fall away. They can't hang with you. They can't go where you're going. God put greatness in you.

Be Like a Teflon Pan

There's a lot of negative chatter these days. With all the social media and other ways to communicate, people can express their opinion so easily and say things that are derogatory, trying to discredit you. The only power that has is the power you give it. If you let it get in you, if you start dwelling on it, that will poison your spirit. Over time, it will change who you are. You'll become defensive, try to prove to people you're okay, try to show that you're not what they said. You're giving them your power. You're engaged in a battle that you're not supposed to be in. The crows are going to crow, making a lot of noise. The chickens are going to peck away with their gossip, jealousy, and criticism. People will have plenty of opinions about how you are to run your life, what you should wear and spend your money on, what you should say and think, how you should raise your children. Successful people are so focused on their goals and dreams that they don't pay attention to the crows. Quit letting that poison get in your spirit. You have a destiny to fulfill. God has given you the gift of life. He could have chosen anyone to be

> *How much time are you wasting by living offended and upset, letting difficult people steal your joy?*

here at this time, but He chose you and me. Let's make the most of this day. How much time are you wasting by living offended and upset, letting difficult people steal your joy? It's time to get focused. Tune out all the negative and run your race with purpose.

In 2 Kings 2, the prophet Elisha was traveling to the city of Bethel. As he was walking along the road, over forty young men came out of the town and started making fun of him because he was bald. They said, "Get out of here, you bald head. Go away, baldy." They were mocking him, dishonoring him, again and again. Elisha had just performed a miracle in the city of Jericho, and he could have gotten upset and been offended. He could have gone after them and straightened them out, but he didn't take the bait. He said, in effect, "I'm going to stay in peace, commit them to God, and let Him fight my battles." He understood they were just a bunch of crows, making a lot of noise, trying to get him distracted, engaged in battles that didn't matter. He kept on going, and as he did, two bears suddenly came out of the woods and mauled forty-two of the young men. When you let God be your vindicator, He'll take care of who's trying to stop you. He'll deal with the disrespect, the jealousy, the people who are doing you wrong. You're an eagle. Don't come down and fight battles that don't matter. You keep soaring, keep doing the right thing, and God will deal with the crows, the chickens, and the turkeys. All that negative chatter is just noise. It cannot stop your destiny.

You're an eagle. Don't come down and fight battles that don't matter.

Psalm 45 says, "God has anointed us with the oil of joy." When you walk in your anointing, there's an oil on you to which nothing can stick. You're like a Teflon pan. When you are disrespected, when people say hurtful things, the good news is that you have a no-stick anointing. You can let an offense go, and it will slide right off you and have no effect. If a coworker leaves you out and plays politics, you could be upset and offended, but you have the oil of joy. You just let it go. If someone is rude to you, jumps down your throat, you could be rude back and give them a piece of your mind, but you're like the Teflon pan. It slides right off, and you go on and enjoy the day. You weren't created to hold on to offenses, to disrespect, to hurtful words. The next time something happens that could upset you, instead of responding the same way you have in the past, try a different approach. "Father, thank You that I've been anointed with the oil of joy. I'm going to stay in peace. I'm going to focus on my goals, knowing that You are fighting my battles."

Don't Give Away Your Power

You can't get rid of the difficult people, but if you respond the right way, they won't keep you from having a blessed, productive, favor-filled day. Are you letting things upset you that don't have to upset you? Are you giving away your power, letting what people do to you determine whether or not you're going to be happy? You need to take back the control of your happiness. Quit putting it in someone else's hands. If you're only going to be happy when other people treat you nice and are kind and say good things, you're giving them your power. You control your happiness. You have to make up your mind that no matter what people do, no matter what they say or how they treat you,

> *You have to make up your mind that no matter what people do, no matter what they say or how they treat you, they're not going to steal your joy.*

they're not going to steal your joy. They may not want to be happy, but they shouldn't keep you from being happy. They may be rude, angry, and disrespectful, but you can't let their issues sour your day. Be like that Teflon pan and let it bounce off you. Enjoy your day despite what they do.

Back when I worked behind the scenes in the television production here at Lakewood, I was at an electronics store to buy some parts for our equipment. I had done this many times before, and I knew that the parts were in the back where only the staff could get them. The man at the counter was on the phone and wasn't in any hurry to get off. He could see me standing there, but he talked for about fifteen minutes. I waited patiently, and when he finally hung up, I thought he would acknowledge me and ask what I needed. But he never looked up. Finally, I asked if he could help me. You would have thought I had just insulted him. He gave me an aggravated look and spoke gruffly, "What do you need?" I asked him for the part I needed. He looked at it and said, "We don't carry that. We never have." I told him that I'd purchased it there many times before. His face got red, smoke started coming out his ears, and he looked as though he was about to explode. He used several curse words before saying, "I told you I don't have it. Now don't ask me for it again!" I wanted to say, "I'll ask you as many times as I feel like asking. I'll call you in the middle of the night if I want to." But I noticed he was bigger than me. I just smiled and said, "No problem. Have a nice day." I didn't mean it, but at least I said it.

You can't stop people from dumping their garbage, but you can keep your lid on. You don't have to let their trash get in you.

I had to make this choice. Was I going to let his poison get in me, to pollute my day, to sour my attitude, to spend my emotional energy being upset and aggravated? Or was

I going to be a Teflon pan and have that no-stick anointing? Was I going to let all the disrespect, the anger, and the poison slide right off me? I decided to let it go. You can't stop people from dumping their garbage, but you can keep your lid on. You don't have to let their trash get in you.

Let It Slide Right Off

Sometimes we have unrealistic expectations. We think we'll have a good day as long as we don't encounter any rude people. As long as our family says nice things, as long as our coworkers perform perfectly, we'll stay in peace. But that's not reality. Difficult people are all around. There will be someone who can steal your joy, offend you, leave you out, or say something that's not true about you. The key is to not try to avoid it; it's to handle it the right way. Don't take the bait. Don't let the offense stay. Don't dwell on the negative comments. Keep yourself oiled up, to where you don't let anything stick. You can live happy, not by avoiding difficult people, but by not taking their garbage. It's by not responding to them when they treat you the wrong way. It's by being an eagle, by rising above the offense, the hurt, the jealousy. When God can trust you to do the right thing when it's hard, there's no limit to how high He will take you.

There was a man walking down the street with his friend to get a newspaper. When they went into the corner store, the clerk in the small newsstand was very cold, inconsiderate, not friendly at all. The man bought the paper and said politely, "I hope you have a great day." As they walked away, the friend said, "Is that clerk always that rude?" He said, "Yes, every morning." The friend replied, "Well, are you always that nice to him?" The man said,

"Yes, every morning." The friend looked puzzled and asked, "Why?" The man answered, "I've made up my mind that I'm not going to let one person ruin my day." As that man did, you have to have a made-up mind that you're not going to let one negative comment ruin your day. You're not going to let a disrespectful coworker, a classmate who's making fun of you, or a driver who cuts you off in traffic to sour your day. Decide ahead of time: *I'm putting on the oil of joy. Whatever comes my way—negative comments, disrespect, rude people—that's going to slide right off me.*

How much more will you enjoy your life if you have this no-stick anointing? You can't control what people do. If they want to be offensive, rude, and hard to get along with, that's their choice. But you can control how you respond. The most powerful thing you can do is to let it slide right off. Don't give it the time of day. Don't think about it anymore, don't relive it, and don't call your friends and tell them what was said or done. Keep your heart pure. Save your emotional energy to live the day to the full, to pursue your dreams, to love your family, to be good to your neighbors. When someone is rude and offensive, don't take that personally. It's not about you; it's that person's own inner struggles. Because they don't like themselves, they don't like you. They're upset over things that have nothing to do with you, and you just happened to enter their story when they're blowing off steam. Stay oiled up and move on. None of that will stop your destiny unless you get distracted and start fighting battles that don't matter, trying to pay people back instead of letting God be your vindicator.

How much more will you enjoy your life if you have this no-stick anointing?

Pass the Nabal Test

This is what David did. In 1 Samuel 25, David and his six hundred men had been living out in the wilderness to keep away from King Saul and his soldiers. A man named Nabal lived in the city of Carmel not far from David. He was very wealthy, with thousands of sheep and goats, but it also says, "Nabal was a mean man. He was dishonest and hard to get along with." By just being around Nabal's property, David and his men had been like of wall of protection from invaders. They were very powerful and could have gotten rid of Nabal's shepherds and taken the flocks, but they were good to Nabal. It was time for sheering the sheep, the harvest season. David sent messengers to Nabal asking for food, since they had been protecting his family and flocks. You would think that Nabal would be grateful that these men had been watching after him, but Nabal was very rude. He said, "Who is this man, David? I never asked him to do anything for me. I don't owe him a penny. Tell him to forget it. I'm not going to give him anything." When David heard that, it set him off. He didn't think about the oil of joy, about the anointing on his life. He didn't sing the psalm that he wrote, "This is the day the Lord has made. Let's be glad." He was furious. He told his men, "Pack up. Strap on your swords. We're going to go take care of Nabal. As surely as I live, not even one male of Nabal's household will be alive by this time tomorrow."

David was offended and angry. He wasn't going to let Nabal get by with insulting him. Yes, there are times when we need to take action and to fight. David fought Goliath and enemy armies. But you have to make sure that battle is between you and your destiny. If not, it's a distraction. David was so wrought up in his emotions that he didn't realize this wasn't a battle he was supposed to fight. How many times are we fighting battles because we're upset and offended because someone did us wrong, but that wasn't a battle between us and our destiny? As with David, it's just our flesh getting riled up, wanting to take matters into our own hands. We were supposed to let it slide off, not dwell on it, and trust God to be our vindicator.

> *How many times are we fighting battles because we're upset and offended because someone did us wrong, but that wasn't a battle between us and our destiny?*

Here's how merciful God is, though. David and four hundred of his men were going full speed ahead to Nabal's house, about to make a mistake that would hinder David's destiny. But Nabal's wife was a wise woman named Abigail. She loaded up two hundred loaves of bread, two containers of wine, two hundred fig cakes, sheep and roasted grain and headed out to meet David. When she saw him, she bowed down low and said, "David, my husband is a fool. He's hardheaded, hot-tempered, and dishonest. He shouldn't have insulted you. I've brought you these gifts hoping you'll forgive him." She went on to say, "David, you are called to be the king of Israel. Why would you even fight with this fool? Why would you waste your time with this stubborn man? Don't let this needless battle be a blemish on your record." She spoke wisdom into David. She was saying, "David, look at who you are. You're the next king. God is going to entrust you with an enduring dynasty, but you're about to blow it by taking revenge on this fool." David came to his senses and said, "Abigail, the Lord God of Israel surely has sent you to me today. For if you had not kept me from carrying out vengeance with my own hands, not one man in your household would be alive."

We're all going to encounter Nabals—people who are rude, hard to get along with, and offensive. I'm asking you what Abigail asked David, "Why are you fighting with a fool?" Why are you

"Why are you fighting with a fool?"

in conflict with someone who's not going anywhere? Why are you upset with the person who cut you off in traffic? You don't even know them. Why are you offended at the coworker? They're not between you and your destiny. They can't stop what God has planned for you. If they don't like you, made negative comments about you, or left you out, that's a test. You can't reach your destiny without dealing with difficult people. Don't get distracted, baited into conflict, into fighting battles that don't matter. Be like that Teflon pan. Don't let any of it stick. God has an awesome future for you, but as the enemy tried with David, he will work overtime to try to get you distracted, offended, and trying to pay people back. Don't take the bait.

Abigail went back home to find her husband partying and very drunk. The next morning, when she told him what she had done to save them, Nabal had a stroke that left him paralyzed. Ten days later he died. When David heard it, he didn't waste any time. Abigail was an intelligent and beautiful woman. He sent word asking her to become his wife, and she agreed. When you let God fight your battles, you'll come out better than you were before. I'm not saying you're going to get an additional spouse as David did, but He'll make it up to you. But if it hadn't been for Abigail, if she had not stopped David from acting on his emotions, we might not be talking about David. If you let people get you upset and offended, and you're focused on paying them back, you can miss your destiny.

When you let God fight your battles, you'll come out better than you were before.

Today, maybe I'm your Abigail. Maybe God sent me to remind you to not let difficult people bait you into conflict, steal your joy, cause you to live frustrated, spending energy on things that don't matter. You can't get away from the Nabals. You may pray one away, but Nabal Jr. will show up tomorrow. You have to make up your mind that difficult people are not going to control you. You're not going to let them offend you, upset you, and push your buttons. Turn those buttons off. Stay in peace. Time is short. We're not always going to be here. Don't waste another minute fighting with the crows, arguing with chickens, debating with turkeys. Be an eagle. Start rising above that. If you do this, I believe and declare that you're not only going to enjoy your life more, but you're going to see vindication, promotion, favor, and breakthroughs. God will take care of your Nabals.

CHAPTER SEVEN

Live in the Present

I know people who lost what they had while going after what they wanted.

So often our mind is either in the past, focused on what didn't work out, who did us wrong, mistakes we've made, or it's in the future, thinking about our goals, worried about our finances, worried about our health. The problem with being in the past or being in the future is that you will miss the present. David says, "This is the day the Lord has made; let us rejoice and be glad in it." Today is a gift from God. Are you fully engaged, making the most of each moment, loving your family, appreciating the simple things in life? Or are you in yesterday? Are you in tomorrow? The reason that some family relationships are not healthy is you come home from work, but you don't really show up. Your mind is somewhere else. You play with your child, but you are in tomorrow, thinking about how you are going to accomplish a goal. Or you go to the office, and your body is there, but your mind is in yesterday, thinking about what you should have done better.

If you're going to be fulfilled, you have to show up for life. You have to be there when you get there. Don't show up and be in the future, worried about how everything is going to work out. Don't show up and be in the past, living in regrets, dwelling on your disappointments. Come into today. Yes, it's good to have goals and vision, but you can't be so focused on what's next that you miss what you have right now. I know people who lost what they had while going after what they wanted. They were so intent on reaching their goal, doing great things, that they took their family for granted. They came home, but they weren't there. They were distracted, thinking about what was next, planning for the future. They never came into the present.

> *If you're going to be fulfilled, you have to show up for life. You have to be there when you get there.*

Stay in the Now

Victoria and I used to travel to India with my father. After we had been married for a couple of years, on the way home from one of our trips, we were going to stop in Paris. My father was going to minister there for a few days. We were so excited, thinking about being in Paris together for our first time. Before we left home, we put an offer in for a house that we really wanted to buy. We had sold our townhome, and we found this place that we loved. It had a nice yard, big trees, and the house was so open and full of light. It was perfect. When we arrived in Paris, the first thing we did was call our realtor and ask if she'd heard anything. She said no, nothing. The next morning, we woke up and called the realtor, "Any news?" Still nothing. During the day, we went out and looked at sights, but the whole time we were talking about the house, believing we were going to get it.

As we walked the streets of Paris, we took pictures of things we wanted to do to our new house. "Here's a front we could put on it. Here's how we could do the landscaping." We were in Paris, but we weren't really there. Our minds were in the future, and all the while we were missing the present. We could have been making the most of the moments, enjoying the sights, taking in that beautiful city, but because we were so focused on what we wanted, we missed what we had. If I could go back in time, I would say, "Joel, enjoy where you are. Be present. At the right time, the doors will open, the opportunities will come, but while you're waiting, stay in the now." What's funny is that when we arrived home, the agent called and said the house had been sold to someone else. I thought, *You mean that I wasted my time in Paris, focused on that house, dreaming about that house, decorating that house, landscaping that house, and we didn't even get it?* Don't lose what you have by going after what you want.

You don't have to go to Paris to miss something great. You can miss your child growing up while you go after what you want. You can miss who your spouse is, all the great things about them, because you're so consumed with your business, with your hobby, with how you're going to fix all those problems. The people in your life are not always going to be there. Don't take them for granted. There will always be plenty of work, plenty of challenges, plenty of problems to solve. Those things will never go away. When you're with your family, give them your time and attention. Life goes by so fast. You look at your little children one day, and the next thing you know they're teenagers, tormenting you...I mean blessing you. When you come home, you need to show up.

The people in your life are not always going to be there. Don't take them for granted.

I charge my cell phone by my bed each night. One morning I

woke up and my phone was dead. I had forgotten to plug it in. It was present but not connected. Sometimes that's the way we are. Victoria and I were present in Paris, but we weren't connected. You can be at work, you're present, but you're not plugged in. Your mind is somewhere else. At home, are you present, eating dinner with the family, but not connected? Are you engaged, making the most of the moments? Or are you in tomorrow, hoping you'll get the contract, worried about your business, wondering how the finances are going to work out? Are you in yesterday, upset over the disappointment, bitter over who hurt you, thinking about what they said? You're missing the beauty of this day. Once we live this day, we can't get it back. Don't take for granted all the good things in your life right now. Get connected. Enjoy where you are. Take time for the people God has given you. The dreams will come to pass in due season. The problems will resolve in God's timing. Worrying about them doesn't make them work out any sooner. Constantly thinking about your goals doesn't make them happen any faster. Stay in the moment.

At home, are you present, eating dinner with the family, but not connected? Are you engaged, making the most of the moments?

Be Present and Connected

It's easy to go on autopilot with our spouse. We've known each other for years, and we're not really engaged anymore. We're just going through the motions. "How was work?" "Fine." "What did you do today?" "Nothing." We used to be connected, but we've been through challenges, had disagreements, and are worn out

In relationships, we change. The person you married at twenty is not the same person at thirty. You can't treat them the same way.

from the pressures of working, raising children, and paying bills. Now we're showing up, but we're not really there. Why don't you get plugged back in? The people in your life can bring you great joy and great fulfillment. When you're present and connected, life is very rewarding.

You have to keep sowing into your relationship. It's not a onetime thing. "We got married, and now we're a couple." The Scripture says, "The two will become one." When you said, "I do," that didn't happen instantly. It takes a lifetime to become one. Victoria and I were talking with some friends one day, kind of joking around. Victoria was laughing and said, "Joel, you don't even know me." I thought, *After thirty-five years of marriage, I don't know you?* I didn't know whether to be excited or afraid. What she was saying is that in relationships, we change. The person you married at twenty is not the same person at thirty. You can't treat them the same way. You have to adapt, adjust, and recognize what they need at this age and this stage. The thirty-year-old is not the same person at fifty. They've grown, they've matured, and they've developed new interests. They have different needs at different stages. You can't put your love on autopilot and treat them the same way. That's why some couples break up. They're not bad people; they've just grown apart. They didn't change. They were present, but they didn't stay connected.

Are you taking time to laugh together, to go on dates, to do new things?

You haven't discovered all the treasures in the person whom God gave you to love. You've seen one stage, but they're going to blossom into new stages. Are you taking time to laugh together, to go on dates, to do new things? Too many couples live in the house, but they're really not home. They sleep in the same bed, but they're not there. Sometimes the reason we're not connected is the past. It's past hurts, past failures, what was said, how we were treated. As long as you're in the past, you'll stay disconnected. You have to let it go. This is a new day. God's mercy is fresh every morning. Come into the present. Life is too short to hold on to hurts, to live upset, focused on what they did wrong. Give that person room to be human. Show them some mercy. No matter who you're in a relationship with, no matter how good they are, at times they're going to disappoint you and let you down. Focus on their good qualities, focus on the reasons you fell in love, how you couldn't live without them.

Give that person room to be human.

When you were dating, that person could do no wrong. You would talk with them on the phone for hours and spend fifteen minutes trying to figure out who was going to hang up first. You laughed and had fun, doing things together. When Victoria and I were dating, I would go anywhere with her. I'd go shopping all day, go to the grocery store together. She could have said, "Let's go see the electrical plant," and I would have gone. It wasn't what we were doing; it was who I was doing it with. I loved being with her. I still do. I was present and connected. She had my full attention.

Over time, life happens. We face challenges, pressures at work, and family members who are difficult. It's easy to let those press us down and we become sour. We don't enjoy our spouse anymore. We don't want to spend time together. We have a list of all the things they've done wrong. The easy way out is to disconnect. "They're not performing up to par, they're not meeting my standards, so I'll check out. I'll go do my own thing, watch TV alone, or hang out with my friends." God didn't put that person in your life by accident. He's given them to you as a gift. Don't wait until they're gone to recognize what you have. Get plugged in. Be kind, be generous, and treat them like a gift. Show them mercy when they make mistakes. Don't hold grudges. You're a team. God put you together. Make your partner better. Encourage them. Help them reach their dreams.

Keep Joy in Your Home

You need to start laughing again, start having fun together. Don't lose the child who's inside you. You should never get so old and so uptight that you can't laugh together. Laughter is like a medicine. It makes us feel better and releases healing throughout our systems. With all the pressures of life and all the negative things in the news, it's easy to become sour and heavy, and everything is a burden. It's easy to take the stress from the office home with you. Keep that tension out of your home. Your home should be a place of peace, a place of joy. One great thing about Victoria is that she loves to laugh and have fun. She keeps the atmosphere of our home joyful. When we laugh, the pressures of life fade and we feel restored and re-energized. We all have challenges. There are things we could be worried about. Our mind could be in the future, trying to figure out a thousand things. It could be in the past, focused on setbacks, things we should have done better. But we do our best to stay in the now, to enjoy each day, to not just be present but connected.

You should never get so old and so uptight that you can't laugh together. Laughter is like a medicine.

One time when I was a little boy, my father and mother had

a disagreement. They didn't see eye to eye. My father felt that my mother had done him wrong. It wasn't anything big, just life. So he decided to give my mother the silent treatment, treating her as though she wasn't worthy of his time or attention. When he came into the kitchen, my mother asked, "Can I get you something to eat?" He said no very curtly, turned and walked away. When she came through the house, he would look the other way and go into another room. This went on all afternoon. He wouldn't give her the time of day. When your mind is in the past, you can't enjoy the present. When you're focused on the hurts, the wrongs, what they said, it's going to keep you from the beauty of the day. I'm not saying someone didn't hurt you or do you wrong, but you can't stay in yesterday and enjoy today. You have to forgive, show mercy, and move forward.

You can't stay in yesterday and enjoy today. You have to forgive, show mercy, and move forward.

My mother decided that she was going to play at his game. She went into a room and hid behind one of the doors. My father walked through the house looking for her, so he could ignore her, but he couldn't find her. He said, "It's hard to ignore someone you can't find." He looked everywhere, in the bathroom, the closet, the utility room. He went out to the garage, then checked the backyard. He started to get worried, thinking, *What if the rapture came and I was left behind?* Finally, he walked past the door where my mother was hiding. She timed it perfectly, jumped on his back, wrapped her legs around his waist, and said, "I'm not getting off until you start talking to me again." My father started laughing so hard that they both fell to the floor, and that was the end of his silent treatment. Keep joy in your home, keep laughter in your relationships. I know there are real issues, but living in strife, holding grudges, and not forgiving will keep you from the new things God has in store.

It's About the Journey

This is what Joseph did in the Scripture. At seventeen years old, God gave him a dream that he was going to lead a nation. But his brothers were jealous of him and threw him into a pit to die, then ended up selling him into slavery. Joseph worked in Egypt as a slave for a high-ranking military officer. He was lied about, falsely accused of a crime, and put in prison. Joseph had plenty of opportunities to live in the past. "How could my brothers treat me this way? I'm going to get revenge. You just wait." He could have lived in the future. "God, You said I was going to lead a nation. What happened?" But you never read that Joseph complained. As a slave, he so excelled that his owner put him in charge of his whole household. In prison, he not only wasn't bitter, but the warden put him in charge of all that was done there. He helped another inmate, interpreting his dream. How could he keep such a good attitude after all he had been through? He stayed in the present. He didn't focus on looking back and say, "That was so unfair." And he didn't focus on looking ahead and say, "God, I'm in prison. When am I going to lead a nation?" He chose to live in the present. His attitude was: *This is where God has me now. I know He's ordering my steps. I'm not going to live upset about the bad breaks. I'm not going to live worried about my future. I'm going to make the most of this day.*

How could he keep such a good attitude after all he had been through?

It's so easy to always be focused on the destination, the dream coming to pass, the problem turning around. You have to do as Joseph did and learn to enjoy where you are while you're on the way to where you're going. Life is not about the destination; it's about the journey. That's where you'll grow. That's where you'll see fulfillment and the favor of God. We have to remember that after we reach a goal, there will be another goal. There'll be another challenge. If we're not careful, we'll rush through the day trying to get to the destination. Slow down and enjoy the journey. Yes, there will be bumps in the road, disappointments, things you don't understand. That's when you have to say, "I'm not looking back. I'm not getting bitter and letting that sour my life. I'm not going to live worried, wondering how it's going to work out. I'm going to stay in the present. I'm going to enjoy where God has me right now, knowing that He will get me to where I'm supposed to be." It takes maturity to enjoy where you are even though you have challenges, even though there are things you don't understand.

Thirteen years after Joseph was thrown into that pit, he was made the prime minister of Egypt. He saw vindication, promotion, and influence greater than he'd ever imagined. What a shame if Joseph had spent those past years discouraged, worried, and frustrated. What God promised you is going to come to pass. The dream He put in your heart is already on the schedule. The question is, How are you spending the time while you're waiting? Are you looking back with regrets and upset? Are you looking forward, wondering why it's not happening? No, stay in the present. Take it one day at a time. You don't have grace for tomorrow. If you're trying to figure out the past twenty years, or the next twenty years, you're going to be frustrated. You have grace for this day. When you get to tomorrow, there will be grace for that day.

You have grace for this day. When you get to tomorrow, there will be grace for that day.

"Joel, I'm worried because I don't see how my situation could ever work out." You're not supposed to. This is what faith is all about. You have to trust that God is in control, that He's planned out all your days, that He knows what's best for you. Instead of fighting where you are, learn to embrace where you are. That's what Joseph did. It wasn't comfortable, he didn't like it, but he embraced it, believing that God was ordering his steps. I don't want you to get ten years down the road and think, *If I had known it was going to turn out this good, I would have enjoyed my life. I would have spent more time with my family. I would have enjoyed raising my children.*

Make the Most of Each Day

I talked to a lady who had been very successful as an executive for a large company. But after she had been there for nineteen years, the company was restructuring, and she was unexpectedly let go. It wasn't because of wrongdoing; her position was no longer needed. She was disappointed, but she knew something else would open up. She has two master's degrees and is very experienced, very personable, a leader in her field. She applied to company after company, even in other states, but no response. No one was interested. She couldn't understand it. A couple of months after she lost her job, her mother became ill and needed someone to take care of her. She decided that she would do it while she was looking for a job. Every day she would go to her mother's house, and they would visit and run errands. Her mother came to her house and helped her fix it up. She had so much fun with her mother and made so many great memories. Ten months later, her mother passed.

Three days after she laid her mother to rest, she started getting one phone call after another from companies that she had applied to months and months before. Not just one offer, but four great offers came in. She accepted a position with more responsibility, more income, and a better environment than in her past position. She said, "It's a position that I enjoy much more than my previous job." Look at how God works. The company unexpectedly letting her go seemed to be a bad break that wasn't fair. Then with her credentials, with all her experience and education, the closed doors, another position not opening up, didn't make sense. She could have been sour and lived upset. "Why is this happening?" But she made the choice to not live in the past, to not let the disappointments steal her joy. She made the choice to not live in the future. "Why won't anything open up? What if I can't find a job?" Instead, she took that time to enjoy where God had her. She made the most of each day. She embraced where she was, believing that God was directing her steps. Had she not done that, she would have missed that time with her mother. Had she lived stressed out, she wouldn't have those memories that she'll forever cherish.

Don't fight where you are; embrace where you are. Make the most of each day. Yes, you may need a job, but don't get so focused on the future that you miss the beauty of this day. Yes, you may be disappointed if a company lets you go, but don't let the past keep you from seeing the good things in your life in the present. God is ordering your steps. Sometimes we don't understand it, and it's not comfortable. But as with Joseph, all the disappointments, delays, and betrayals are a part of God's plan to get you to the throne. God is going to get you to your destiny. He's going to work all things for your good. While you're waiting, when you don't see anything happening, things aren't turning around, trust Him enough to enjoy your life. See the good in each day. Be grateful for what you have. There's a song that says, "It's a beautiful day, don't let

Don't fight where you are; embrace where you are.

While you're waiting, when you don't see anything happening, things aren't turning around, trust Him enough to enjoy your life.

it get away." Once we live this day, we can't get it back. Are you living it in tomorrow, focused only on your dreams? Are you living in yesterday, focused on what didn't work out, when all the while God has you at this place for a reason? There's a blessing in disguise. There's someone with whom you can connect. There's a test you can pass. If Joseph had been bitter, he would have never helped the man who had been the chief butler to Pharaoh. The butler is the one who helped open the door for him.

Enjoy

The Scripture says, "Make the most of this day." It doesn't say to make the most of yesterday or to make the most of tomorrow. What are you doing with today? Are you embracing where you are, or are you fighting where you are? Are you present and connected, or are you present and disengaged? When life called the roll today, did you show up, passionate, enjoying your family, looking forward to another great day? "Joel, I would, but I've had some disappointments. People have done me wrong. My dream hasn't worked out." How do you know those things are not leading you to your destiny? God is ordering your steps. It may not be good, but He

When life called the roll today, did you show up, passionate, enjoying your family, looking forward to another great day?

wouldn't have allowed it if it was going to stop your purpose. Don't get twenty years down the road and see it all come together, then have to say, "Wow! I spent so much of my life worried, not enjoying my family, mad at the people who did me wrong." Let it go. It's all a part of the process. These are tests we have to pass.

We can get to our destination while enjoying the journey, seeing God's favor despite the opposition. Or we can get there worried, sour, and upset. I'm asking you to live in the present. One day at a time. Yes, it's good to have goals and keep your vision in front of you, but don't let what hasn't happened to frustrate you. Make up your mind that you're going to enjoy each day, enjoy your family, enjoy the people you work with, enjoy the beauty of creation. Take time to smell the roses. All through the day, it's good to take a few deep breaths and just breathe in God's goodness. Breathe in where you are. Don't be trying to rush through one part of the day just to get to the next. Take time to enjoy the present.

All through the day, it's good to take a few deep breaths and just breathe in God's goodness.

One thing the pandemic did was to help us have a new perspective. Sometimes we would complain about "normal." "I don't want to go to work, or get these kids ready for school, or drive in the traffic, or cook dinner and have to clean up." But after the pandemic shut everything down month after month, and we couldn't go to work, couldn't send our kids to school, and couldn't leave the house, normal looked pretty good. Sometimes, when something is taken away and you get it back, you tend to appreciate it more. Maybe that job we didn't like wasn't so bad. Maybe the traffic doesn't have to frustrate us. Believe it or not, that person at work who used to get on our nerves, maybe we're looking forward to seeing the jerk…I mean the man. We have a new perspective.

We're alive, we have breath to breathe, and we have strength to get out of bed. We have a family to love, we have a place to live, we have peace in our mind, and we have the favor of God.

When you realize this day is a gift, you will live it to the full. Your joy and happiness are not dependent on your past nor based on your future. But you will say with David, "This is the day the Lord has made. I'm not going to just drag through it. I'm going to rejoice and be glad in it. I'm not just going to be present; I'm going to be connected. I'm going to make the most of it." If you do this, I believe and declare that you're going to have better relationships, you're going to have more joy and fulfillment. As with Joseph, negative situations are about to turn around, promotion is coming, healing, breakthroughs, the fullness of your destiny.

CHAPTER EIGHT

Let It Go

When you bury negative emotions, they never die.

We all go through disappointments, things that are not fair. It's easy to hold on to the hurts, to think about the negative things people have said to us, to relive the offense. We get up in the morning and it's the first thing that comes to mind. We don't realize how much that's affecting us. It's souring our attitude, draining our energy, and limiting our creativity. If you're going to fulfill your destiny, you have to get good at letting things go. Jesus says, "Offenses will come." He didn't say they might come. He didn't say that if you're a good person, if you're nice all the time, nobody will do you wrong. He says that disappointments will come. Betrayals will come. Things that are not fair will come. How you deal with these offenses, how you handle the hurts, will determine whether you move forward and see the new things God has in store or whether you get stuck, bitter over what didn't work out.

I've heard it said if you don't heal from emotional wounds, you will bleed on people who had nothing to do with it. How many people are living wounded over how they were raised, a friend who walked away, or a business partner who cheated them? Instead of

Until you get well, you can't develop healthy relationships. Until you stop carrying the hurt, you could easily live angry and upset with a chip on your shoulder. Until you let go of what didn't work out, that wound is going to hinder you wherever you go.

letting it go, they replay it over and over in their mind, reliving all the hurt. Then they wonder why they don't have good relationships. It's because they haven't healed. They're living out of a wounded place. God brings a new person into their life, somebody great, but they're so insecure. They don't feel valuable or attractive. This new person has to keep them fixed, has to go overboard to make sure they know how great they are. The problem is, that's not sustainable. Until you get well, you can't develop healthy relationships. Until you stop carrying the hurt, you could easily live angry and upset with a chip on your shoulder. Until you let go of what didn't work out, that wound is going to hinder you wherever you go.

If you're still wounded over a position you lost unfairly in one company, you'll go to a new company being defensive, on edge, and not friendly. You'll treat your new boss and coworkers based on what you've been through, but they had nothing to do with it. It's much more freeing when you learn to let things go. It wasn't fair. That's okay, because God will be your vindicator. He'll take care of who did you wrong. It's not your job to pay people back. They hurt you once; don't let them continue to hurt you by holding on to it. You lost a loved one, which I know is painful, and it's healthy to go through a season of mourning, but you can't hold on to the hurt. Living in mourning is going to keep new doors from opening. You have to heal so you can see new relationships and new opportunities.

Perpetual Forgiveness

In the Scripture, Peter asked Jesus how many times he should forgive someone who did him wrong. It's funny because Peter was known to be offensive. He's the one who cursed out the young lady in the courtyard after Jesus was arrested and was standing before the Sanhedrin. He cut off the ear of the servant of the high priest trying to defend Jesus. Yet it was Peter who asked, "Jesus, should I forgive them seven times?" The Jewish law said to forgive three times, so he more than doubled it. He thought, *Jesus, I'm growing. I've come a long way.* Jesus said, "Peter, seven is good, but I want you to forgive them seventy times seven." It wasn't about the number. Jesus was showing us a principle. He was saying, "I want you to live in a continual process of forgiveness." This is not something you do every once in a while. Forgiveness should be a part of our life on a daily basis. He was setting a system in place so that we wouldn't hold on to hurts, offenses, and disappointments. He knew that practically every day we would have these opportunities. The quicker you let things go, the easier it is.

Forgiveness should be a part of our life on a daily basis.

In the Lord's Prayer, Jesus told us to pray, "Give us this day our daily bread, and forgive us our trespasses, as we forgive those who trespass against us." He was saying that every day we should be ready to forgive. It doesn't have to be big things. It can be the person who cut you off in traffic. Let it go. Don't let that sour your day. Your time is valuable. That's a distraction that's trying to get you off course, trying to get you offended over something that doesn't matter. When that clerk is rude to you at the grocery store, just smile and move on. I've learned that life is full of wounded

How much better would your relationships be if you would get emotionally healthy, if you would let go of what people said, forgive the person who did you wrong, and quit reliving the hurts?

people, people who haven't dealt with the negative things in their past. At times, they'll be disrespectful, they'll say things they shouldn't, and they'll do things that are hurtful. You can't stop the offense from coming, but you can keep it from getting inside you. How much time are you spending offended, bitter, holding a grudge? How much more could you accomplish if you start letting things go? How much better would your relationships be if you would get emotionally healthy, if you would let go of what people said, forgive the person who did you wrong, and quit reliving the hurts?

In the Scripture, this is where David excelled. He was an expert at letting go of offenses. When David was a teenager, his father, Jesse, didn't believe in him, looked down on him, and didn't affirm him. When the prophet Samuel came to their house to choose one of Jesse's eight sons as the next king of Israel, Jesse didn't even call David in from the shepherds' fields. He thought David was too small, too young, and not that talented as compared to his older brothers. He didn't give David a chance. It was only after Samuel didn't choose one of the other sons that David was called in. David could have lived bitter, with a chip on his shoulder. He felt the sting of rejection from his own family. His brothers made fun of him. When David delivered a provision of food to his brothers on the battlefield, his oldest brother, Eliab, tried to belittle him in front of other soldiers. He said, "David, what are you doing here, and what did you do with those few sheep you're supposed to be taking care of?" He was condescending and sarcastic. David could have been offended and upset, but the Scripture says, "David turned and walked away." He knew the importance of letting things go. Had David not done this, he would never have seen Goliath. Had he stayed there and tried to straighten out his brother, we wouldn't be talking about him.

The truth is, David's father wasn't fair. It wasn't right to leave David out in the fields. His brothers were demeaning and belittling. But you can't make people do what's right. It's a test. Are you holding on to the offense, letting the betrayal, or what they said, or how they treated you cause you to be sour? Do you wake up thinking about it? Or are you going to let it go and move forward into your destiny? There is a Goliath waiting for you that will take you to a new level, but you have to get past the offense, past the rejection, past what someone said. My prayer is that we will do as David did and live with this perpetual forgiveness, that we'll develop a habit of forgiving daily. Then, when offenses come, they will bounce off us like water off a duck's back. If a family member doesn't believe in you, that's unfortunate, but that's not going to keep you from doing great things. If a coworker tries to make you look bad and embarrass you, most people would be upset, start a fight, and pay them back, but you're a David. You recognize that it's a distraction. You let it go, knowing that God will take care of your enemies. One way that God vindicates you is to promote you in the presence of your enemies. He doesn't do it in private, but in public, so that those who left you out, discounted you, or tried to make you feel small will see you promoted, honored, in a position of greater influence.

Are you holding on to the offense, letting the betrayal, or what they said, or how they treated you cause you to be sour?

When David defeated Goliath, the whole Israelite army was

in awe. The city was cheering. Even the Philistines, the opposition, couldn't believe what David had done. God knows how to lift you up when other people are trying to push you down. Don't let that offense in. Start letting things go quickly. Don't think about it for a week and then you'll do it. If you don't let in the offenses in the first place, you won't have to get over so many emotional wounds. David could have woken up each morning and thought about how his father mistreated him, how he left him out. He could have thought about how his brothers were demeaning. But that bitterness, anger, and self-pity would have stopped his destiny. When the offense comes up, don't go there. Keep your mind on the positive. Think on things that are good, wholesome, and uplifting. To think about something negative that was said about you, to relive how the person walked away, to rehearse all the pain and go back over all the sorrow is going to keep you from healing. Let it go. That's in the past. God saw what happened. He heard what they said. He knows what you lost. If you let it go, He'll make it up to you. He'll give you beauty for those ashes.

> *If you don't let in the offenses in the first place, you won't have to get over so many emotional wounds.*

Forgive for Your Own Sake

A friend of mine grew up in a single-parent home. When he was five years old, his father walked out of his life and wouldn't have anything to do with him. As a little boy, he longed to see his dad, but his dad wouldn't return his mother's calls. In his teens, he would send letters to his father as well as birthday and Father's Day cards. He wanted his father's approval so badly, just to know that he cared, but he never heard a word. He felt the rejection. Thoughts told him that he wasn't good enough, that there was something wrong with him, but he didn't go there. He didn't let in the bitterness or the self-pity. He said what the psalmist says, "Even if my mother and father forsake me, God will adopt me as His very own child." Despite the injustice and unfairness, when you live in a state of perpetual forgiveness as he did, it's amazing how you'll still be happy, you'll still enjoy your life, and you'll still do great things.

When he was in his thirties, his father finally agreed to see him. He was so excited. It was a dream come true. He flew to another city, knocked on the door, but a lady answered and said, "I'm sorry. Your father has changed his mind. He's not going to see you." I thought my friend would have been devastated, but he said, "Joel, it didn't really bother me. I had already prepared that if he wouldn't see me, I was going to let it go and move on." It has not stopped this young man. He's happily married, has four beautiful children, and is very successful. I would never have known that he didn't have an amazing childhood. When you learn to let things go, disappointments, unfair people, how you were raised, and bad breaks can't stop you. You'll keep rising higher, seeing the goodness of God.

I've met other people who have been through things similar to my friend. They're bitter, angry, have a chip on their shoulder, and are stuck in life. What's the difference? They hold on to everything. You can't stop it from coming, but you can keep the poison from getting inside. When you bury negative emotions, they never die. You can't bottle up the anger, the hurt, the betrayal, and think that those are not going to affect you. "Joel, I can't forgive them. You don't know what they did. I can't let it go. They hurt me too badly." But you're not forgiving and letting it go for their sake; you're doing it for your sake. That poison is contaminating your life. When you release it, you'll step into new levels of freedom, joy, and victory.

You can't bottle up the anger, the hurt, the betrayal, and think that those are not going to affect you.

Get the Contaminants Out

There was a professional boxer who was the middle weight champion of the world back in the 1990s. He was known for his aggressiveness in the ring. He fought with such anger and viciousness, almost as though he was out of control. After one fight, a reporter asked him why he fought with such aggression, how he could be that driven. The reporter was expecting a standard answer, such as, "I'm just very competitive, and I love to box." But the boxer said the reason he fought with such anger and such hostility was because his father was abusive. He mistreated his mother and fought with her. Their home was very violent. His father had told him that he would never amount to anything. When he was ten years old, his father abandoned the family, and he never saw him again. He said, "When I step into the ring, I picture my father's face on my opponent. I have so much hatred toward him, I just explode."

I thought about the difference between my friend and this boxer. Both had betrayals, both had rejection, but one is living healthy, with great children, and being blessed. The other is angry, violent, and bitter. The difference is that one learned to let things go, and the other chose to hold on. Yes, the boxer had success on the outside, but if you're poisoned inside, it's going to spoil every victory. Is there something you need to let go of? Is there bitterness and anger about how someone treated you or what didn't work out? Don't do as the boxer did and let that poison the rest of your life. It wasn't right what they did, but you're forgiving so you can be free. You're letting it go so you can see beauty for the ashes.

> *If you're poisoned inside, it's going to spoil every victory.*

Years ago, there was toxic waste that needed to be discarded, but nobody knew what to do with it. They had never had to get rid of something that toxic and dangerous. After studying it and getting different opinions, a company built big metal containers like you see on a ship, and they put the toxic waste in it. They went to great lengths to make sure it was sealed very tightly, and the toxic waste wouldn't get out. Then they buried these containers deep in the ground. They were so relieved that they finally got rid of it. They thought they were done, but forty years later, the containers started leaking. The toxin was contaminating the soil, the water, the air, forcing people to move away. The problem was that the waste was too toxic to bury.

There are some things you can't bury, such as anger, and think it's not going to affect you. You can't bury bitterness, hatred, and rejection and not have it leak out. That's too toxic. That poison, at some point, will contaminate not just your dreams, your attitude, and your vision, but it will affect the people around you. The best thing you can do is get that toxic waste out of you. Let it go. You have to give it to God. "God, I forgive them for what they did. I let go of the hurts, what I lost, what I didn't get. I trust You to make it up to me."

> *You can't bury bitterness, hatred, and rejection and not have it leak out. That's too toxic.*

That company never dreamed that years later they would be dealing with the same toxic problem, but by this time the contamination had spread and become worse. If they had disposed of it properly the first time, they wouldn't have had this difficulty. The good news is that it's not too late to do something about it. You don't have to live with that contamination inside. Let it go. Forgive the person who hurt you, forgive the parent for what they didn't give you. Let go of the disappointment, the dream that didn't work out. Let go of the guilt, the shame, the regret, the remorse. I've known people who have carried guilt for so long that they've suffered nervous breakdowns. They are worn down and can barely function. You can't keep that bottled up and reach your potential.

Don't Let the Poison In

David went to the palace to work as one of King Saul's armorbearers. For a time, Saul was proud of David and loved him like a son, but over time Saul became jealous of David. He could see the anointing and favor on David's life. Instead of being happy for David, Saul wanted to get rid of him. While David was playing the harp for Saul, trying to make Saul feel better, Saul threw a spear at David and barely missed him. David had to flee for his life. He had done nothing but good for Saul. He had honored and served him, but in return Saul tried to kill him. David spent years living on the run, hiding in caves, with Saul and his men chasing after him. At one point, David could have killed Saul. He snuck up on Saul and his men while they were sleeping, but he wouldn't harm Saul. Despite David being good to Saul, Saul never changed his mind. He wouldn't have him back in the palace. After several years, Saul was killed in a battle, and David was made the king.

When David heard that Saul was gone, you would think he would have been relieved and happy. Finally, this man who had made his life miserable, caused him heartache, and caused him to live where he couldn't pursue his dreams was no longer there. Surely, David would call his men together and have a big party. But the Scripture says that when David learned Saul was killed, he wept and wrote a song honoring him, saying, "How beloved and how gracious was Saul." No wonder David rose so high. He learned to let things go. Can you imagine writing a song that honors your biggest enemy, the one who tried to keep you down, saying how beloved they are? A key to David's success is that he didn't let the toxins get inside. He didn't bury the things that weren't fair, the injustices, the anger, or the hurt. He turned it all over to God. Even years later, when he was sitting in the palace, the greatest leader of that day or maybe of any day, having conquered all kinds of territory and seen God's favor in great ways, David said to his staff, "Is there anyone still alive from the house of Saul that I can bless?" He still had no bitterness toward Saul. He was still being good to a man who hadn't been good to him. Who knows where God will take you if you just let things go when you have every right to be angry and bitter? I'm not saying it's easy to let go of the hurt, of the pain when someone left you, or when you lost someone valuable. But it's more difficult to deal with the toxins inside than it is to let things go. It's not always easy to forgive, but it's harder to deal with the poison of unforgiveness. It's not easy to move forward after a disappointment, but it's harder to stay stuck in defeat and mediocrity.

A key to David's success is that he didn't let the toxins get inside.

It's not always easy to forgive, but it's harder to deal with the poison of unforgiveness.

Coach Rudy Tomjanovich was a great basketball player and became the Hall of Fame coach of the Houston Rockets. During an NBA game when he was twenty-five years old, a fight broke out between two players. Rudy ran full speed to break them up just as one of the players turned and threw a punch as hard as he could without looking. The punch hit Rudy square in the face, and it became known as "the punch heard around the world." It fractured his skull, broke his nose and cheekbones, and resulted in spinal fluid leaking out. It almost took Rudy's life. Months later, while he was recovering, reporters asked him about the player who hit him and what he thought. Everyone was waiting for his response. Surely, he would be angry and bitter over what was so wrong. Rudy didn't miss a beat. He told how he had already forgiven the player, that he wasn't angry or upset. The reporters were puzzled and said, "This man almost ended your life. He put you through all these months of pain. How could you possibly forgive him?" Rudy said, "I knew the only way I could move forward was to let it go. I didn't forgive just for his sake. I did it so that I could be free."

Maybe you've had bad breaks. You weren't treated right. It wasn't fair. I'm not asking you to do the other person a favor; I'm asking you to do yourself a favor. Forgive so you can be free. Forgive so you can reach your potential. Forgive so you can see the beauty for ashes. Don't bury the toxins. Don't bury what they did. Those negative feelings are alive. They can't be contained. You have to give it to God. Trust Him to make it up to you. You weren't created to live with poisons weighing you down, contaminating your vision. You will rise so much higher if you get free from that.

Forgive so you can be free. Forgive so you can reach your potential.

Give Birth to Something Better

David had another great disappointment. His newborn baby became very sick. Because he had committed adultery with Bathsheba, God told him the baby wouldn't live. David went home and prayed, asking God to change His mind and heal his child. For seven days he wouldn't eat, wouldn't see anyone, and was consumed with this baby, asking for a miracle. Unfortunately, the baby died. David's advisers were so concerned that if they told him, he might fall apart. They didn't know what to do. David overheard them and asked what was wrong. When he found out the baby had died, the Scripture says he got up off the floor, washed his face, changed his clothes, then went to the Tabernacle to worship. When he returned to the palace, he asked for a meal and ate. His men were so surprised. They said, "David, when the baby was alive, you were so distraught. But now that the baby is gone, you seem as though you're fine." David responded, "I cannot bring the baby back, but one day I will go to be where he is." David could have been bitter and said, "God, why didn't You answer my prayer? I've served You. I did the right thing when Saul was chasing me. I've tried to honor You, and now this happened." No, David knew to let it go. "I don't understand it, God, but You're still on the throne. I know You still have good things in store for me." There's a lot in life we're not going to understand. You can't get caught up in the whys. Part of faith is trusting when it doesn't make sense.

A year later, David's wife had another baby. They named him Solomon. He became the heir to the throne, the king after David, and the wisest man who ever lived. Had David stayed in despair, shame, and condemnation, had he not washed his face and let go of the disappointment, he would never have seen the king who

Had David stayed in despair, shame, and condemnation, had he not washed his face and let go of the disappointment, he would never have seen the king who was coming.

was coming. In difficult times, when you could be bitter with yourself over something you've done, if you just let it go and keep trusting God, as David did, you'll give birth to a king. You'll give birth to something greater than what you've imagined, something where you don't think about what you've lost.

I heard a story about an eagle that swooped down and picked up a mole that was crawling on the ground. This was unusual because eagles rarely pick up and eat moles. It grabbed it with its talons and held it close to its chest. As the eagle was flying, holding the mole so close, it began to tire and get weak. It flew lower and lower, and finally it had to land. Once on the ground, the eagle lost all its strength, fell over, and died. The mole scurried away unharmed. It was very puzzling until a veterinarian discovered that the mole had very subtly bit into the eagle's chest, punctured the eagle's heart, and caused it to lose blood pressure. Apparently the eagle couldn't feel it and held the mole until it eventually passed.

Are you holding on to something that you don't realize is killing you? If there's anger, bitterness, guilt, or shame, that's draining the life out of you. That's taking your joy, your peace, your creativity. How much higher could you fly, how much further could you go, if you got rid of the things that you're not supposed to be carrying? Today can be a turning point. Do you know what's more powerful than negative emotions? A decision. It's when you decide to let it go, when you wash your face as David did, when you say "I forgive"

Today can be a turning point.

as Rudy did. Then you're moving toward the king that's in your future. You may have buried some toxins; you may be carrying some things that you shouldn't. You can release them right now. This is your time to be free. If you do this, I believe and declare that you're about to soar to new heights, new doors are about to open, and new friendships, healing, restoration, and breakthroughs are on the way.

CHAPTER NINE

Nothing to Prove

Rest in who God made you to be.

Too often we're trying to get our worth from what we do. So much of it is about how well we think we're performing. We ask ourselves, "Am I a good enough parent? Am I talented enough, strong enough, successful enough?" We think if we work harder, outperform our coworker, outdress our friend, or outdrive our neighbor, we'll feel good about ourselves. We live in a proving mode with this need to impress. The problem is that we're getting our value from the wrong place. If you don't know who you are, a child of the Most High God, you'll spend your energy trying to get other people to validate you. When you're secure in who God made you to be, when you're comfortable with your gifts, content with your looks, and happy with your personality, you don't go around competing with others, being jealous of a friend who's more talented, or living to impress a cousin who's more attractive. You know you're one of a kind, a masterpiece, made in the image of God.

When you know who you are, you won't live in a proving mode, trying to impress people or get your value from what others think.

You don't go around thinking, *Do they accept me? Do they compliment me? Do they approve me? If not, I'll work harder. I'll prove to them that I'm good enough.* No, you don't need their applause. Having them validate you is not going to move you toward your destiny. Having others cheer you on is nice, but if you're getting your worth from that, you'll feel devalued and not good enough when they quit giving it. You'll have to work harder, do more to impress them, and stay on that treadmill. You're doing all this work but not going anywhere. Take the pressure off. You have nothing to prove. Your destiny is not contingent on others liking you. Their disapproval is not keeping you from your purpose. It's a distraction. You're spending time and energy trying to impress, to outperform, to show them that you're good enough, when, in fact, you're already good enough. You've already been approved. God created you in His own image. Now run your race. They may be very talented and successful. Celebrate them. You're not competing with them. You don't have to prove to them that you're talented, too. You have gifts that they don't have. Be confident in who God made you to be.

Having others cheer you on is nice, but if you're getting your worth from that, you'll feel devalued and not good enough when they quit giving it.

Your Value Comes from Who You Are

I talked with a man whose father was very hard on him, very condescending when he was growing up. His father told him that he was never going to amount to anything. Now this man is in his forties, working night and day, trying to prove to his father that he was wrong, trying to prove that he is talented and successful. His father still hasn't acknowledged his success or complimented him. I told him what I'm telling you. You don't have to convince anyone that you're good enough. That person doesn't control your destiny. That's a distraction. You're trying to impress someone who's never going to be impressed. No matter what you do, it's not going to be good enough. Your job is not to change other people's minds; your job is to run your race. Don't get your value from people; get your value from God. Any time we're trying to prove our worth, the root cause is insecurity. Your value should come from who you are, not from what you do or what you have. If not, there will always be a voice saying, "You don't measure up. You need to be stronger, skinnier, taller, wealthier, more talented, a better parent."

You don't have to convince anyone that you're good enough.

It's very freeing when you understand that you have nothing to prove. You don't have to prove to others that you're good enough. You may have a neighbor who's a supermom. She does everything for her children, including sewing their clothes. After school, they do arts and crafts, then Little League, then ballet practice, then singing lessons, then pilot lessons, then Algebra Three. They do field trips on the weekends, and they study Chinese on Fridays. You don't have to keep up with her to prove that you're a good mother. She may have been graced for that. She's walking in her anointing, her calling, her gifting. (I feel sorry for her kids.) But you're not competing with her. If you go into a proving mode and try to outperform her, feeling less-than because you're not like her, all that's going to do is wear you out and take your joy. You're trying to prove something that you don't have to prove. You've entered a race that you're not competing in. Walk in your anointing. You don't have to keep up with other people. If you're getting your value from how you measure up to your peers, you'll live in a proving mode, working harder, trying to impress. "Am I as talented as my coworker? Am I as successful as my cousin?" That's a never-ending cycle. Get off that treadmill. You have nothing to prove. You don't have to be better than your neighbor, more talented than your friend, or skinnier than your cousin. That's not your race. You're not competing with them; you're competing with yourself. Be the best you that you can be.

We all know women who are naturally a size fourteen and other women who are naturally a size six. It's not about their discipline, diet, or willpower; it's about genetics. It's about who God made you to be. If you're competing in a race you're not supposed to be in, you're going to live frustrated. If you didn't eat for three years, you still would not be a size six. Why are you competing in a race that was never designed for you? What are you trying to prove? Do you think that when you get small enough, strong enough, or successful enough, then you can feel good about yourself? Get out of that race. You can feel good about who you are right now. You are in a class all by yourself. When God made you, He threw away the mold. He stepped back and said, "That was good. Another masterpiece. Made in My image." He put His DNA in you. Who said you don't look good? Who said you're not talented enough? Who said you need to be taller, more creative, or have a better personality? Don't believe those lies. Quit comparing, quit competing, and run your race.

Do you think that when you get small enough, strong enough, or successful enough, then you can feel good about yourself?

Run Your Race

When our children were small, most of my siblings homeschooled their children. I asked my sister Lisa about it. She said, "When you send them off to school, that's eight hours a day that they're being influenced by someone else." I thought, *That's eight hours that I get a break.* We felt the pressure to be like them. Sometimes we do things with the wrong motives. *I'm going to homeschool my children so you won't look down on me. I'm going to prove that I'm a good parent, too.* You have to follow your own heart. When you compare yourself with others, you'll start competing. The problem is that you're not running their race. The grace on their life is going to be different from the grace on your life. It's not a one size fits all. If you think you have to do what they're doing or else you're going to look less-than, you're going to get distracted from your destiny. You don't have to prove that you're just as strong, just as committed, or just as talented. We decided to put our children in school, and they did great for the first four or five years. Eventually, when we started traveling a lot, we did homeschool them. The point is to run your race. You have nothing to prove.

The grace on their life is going to be different from the grace on your life. It's not a one size fits all.

You don't have to prove to God that you're worthy. He's already made you worthy. You don't have to prove that you deserve His goodness. He knew every mistake you would make, every fault, every weakness, and He's already accepted and approved you. Quit trying to win over His approval. Quit thinking that if you read your Bible enough, pray enough, quote enough Scripture, serve enough, and give enough that you'll be good enough. Rest in who

He made you to be. You're not supposed to live striving, pressured, hoping you can measure up, and maybe you can earn His blessing. You don't have to earn it. When He breathed life into you, He put His blessing on you. You're already qualified. Take the pressure off and walk in that blessing.

Rest in who He made you to be.

You weren't created to live in this proving mode of trying to impress others, to outperform your coworker, not feeling good about yourself unless you're outachieving others. Living to impress other people will keep you from your destiny. That's time and energy you need for your dreams and goals. You may impress some people. You may win their approval. They may compliment you and say, "You're looking great today. You are so successful." Praise from people is nice, but not if it just feeds our ego. We should live to impress God. He controls the universe. Promotion is not going to come from the people you impress. Proving to your friend that you're talented and successful may make you feel good, but they don't open doors, they don't part Red Seas, and they don't line up favor or divine connections. Instead of trying to impress people, we should spend our time impressing God.

Guard Your Motives

When you're secure in who God made you to be, you don't feel less-than because you can't do what somebody else does. God has given us different gifts. I don't feel inferior because my brother is a medical doctor and I don't have a college degree. I realize Paul got the brains, but I got the looks. My security is not in how I perform, in what I do, what I wear, or what title is behind my name. My security is in

When you're secure in who God made you to be, you don't feel less-than because you can't do what somebody else does.

the fact that I am a child of Almighty God. I say this with humility, but I realize I'm a masterpiece. I'm fearfully and wonderfully made. I'm equipped, empowered, approved, and anointed. You have to get your value from who you are and not what you do. Otherwise, you'll spend your whole life competing with others, trying to prove your importance, trying to convince them to be for you. "Look at the car I drive. Look at the business I've built. Look at my position. Look at what great shape I'm in." That's all good, but it's superficial. If it changes, your self-worth will change.

Years ago, a friend invited me to come to his house after we played basketball at the gym, so I jumped in the car with him. He had a really beautiful sports car. As we were driving to his house, I noticed he was taking the long way. He could have saved a few miles taking the direct route. I asked why he didn't go the easy way. He said, "My ex-girlfriend lives on this street. I always drive by to make sure she sees what she's missed out on." They had been broken up for almost ten years, but every chance he got, he still went out of his way to prove that she was missing out, to prove that he was successful, to prove that he was happy without her. What's funny is that he found out later she had moved across town years earlier. All that time he was driving by, proving his point, she wasn't even there.

I wonder how many times we're trying to prove something to someone, and the person isn't even paying attention. We're trying to impress people who don't even care. We're competing with someone who doesn't even know we're competing. Yes, it's good to have goals, it's good to have people who challenge us and inspire us to go further, but we're not going to be blessed if our motives are not pure. When our motive in trying to impress someone is to feed our ego, to pay them back, to show them how great we are, or to make up for our lack of self-worth, that's a dead-end street. Let God fight your battles. Let Him promote you. Let Him vindicate you. His favor upon us is not so we can prove that we're talented or as good as someone else. It's to fulfill our assignment. It's to advance the kingdom.

> *I wonder how many times we're trying to prove something to someone, and the person isn't even paying attention.*

Who are you trying to impress? Who are you competing with? How much time and energy are you spending trying to feel good enough, talented enough, smart enough, worthy enough? It's not worth it. Try a different approach. Come out from under the pressure of striving and working. You have nothing to prove. What people think about you doesn't determine your destiny. Accomplishing more is nice, but it's not going to make you more valuable. Your income may increase, but your value is not going to increase. Don't get baited into being competitive, trying to outperform, thinking that's going to give you more worth. Run your race. Stay focused on what you're called to do. Don't live for other people's applause; live for God's applause.

> *Who are you trying to impress? Who are you competing with?*

You Can't Make Yourself More Valuable

In Luke 3, Jesus was being baptized in the Jordan River by John the Baptist. When He came up out of the water, "The Holy Spirit descended on him in bodily form like a dove, and a voice came from Heaven and said, 'This is My beloved Son, in whom I am well pleased.'" What's interesting is that Jesus had not started His ministry. He had never healed anyone, never opened a blind eye, never turned water into wine. Yet His Father said, "I am well pleased with You." God was pleased with who Jesus was and not with what He could do. His value didn't come from His performance. I could understand God saying He was pleased after Jesus raised Lazarus from the dead, after He multiplied the five loaves and fed the multitude, after He cured the lepers. But God doesn't base your value on what you do, on how well you perform, on how talented you are, or how many people look up to you. It's based on the fact that you're His child. He breathed life into you. He made you in His own image. There's nothing you can do that will make you more valuable. No matter how well you perform or how successful you are, it doesn't change how God sees you right now.

> *God doesn't base your value on what you do, on how well you perform, on how talented you are, or how many people look up to you.*

We may think, *If I could perform better, if I could be more disciplined, if I could become more successful, then God would smile down on me, then He would show me His favor.* But He's already smiling on you. He's already crowned you with His favor. Sure, you may have some areas you need to improve in. We all do. But that doesn't change your value. When God looks at us, He says, "There's Charles. He's My son, whom I love, and I am well pleased with him. There's Nancy, Maria, and Rhonda. They are My daughters, whom I love, and I am well pleased with them." When you understand that God is pleased with you, it doesn't really matter what other people think about you. If they are not for you, if they try to discredit you and withhold their approval, big deal. They didn't breathe life into you. They didn't know you before you were formed in your mother's womb. They didn't call you, equip you, and anoint you.

Why are you trying to prove to people who you are when God has already said He is well pleased with you? Why are you spending time and energy trying to impress your neighbor, or prove to the person who walked away that you really are okay, or prove to a coworker that you are talented? You don't have anything to prove. They don't control your destiny. They can't stop what God has purposed for your life. Get your eyes off people, off your faults, and off any thoughts that you don't measure up. You are approved, you are accepted, and you are anointed. Now step into your destiny.

Why are you trying to prove to people who you are when God has already said He is well pleased with you?

Pass the Test

After that great moment when Jesus was baptized and God the Father announced that He was pleased with Him, the Scripture says, "The Spirit led Jesus into the wilderness to be tempted." On one side of the Jordan River, it was lush and green, with abundant fruits and vegetables, so fertile and beautiful. On the other side, it was barren and dry, hot and dusty, with nothing green and growing. You would think that after this incredible moment, surely the Spirit would take Jesus into the nice, comfortable, fertile land, so He could start His ministry with ease. But it was just the opposite. He was led into the desert to be tempted. You can be in the desert by design. Sometimes God will lead you into the wilderness. The good news is that God will not take you into something that He's not going to bring you out of. Stay faithful in the wilderness. Pass the test. Keep doing the right thing.

One of the tests that Jesus had to pass in the desert was not proving Himself. After forty days, the enemy came to Jesus and said, "If you are the Son of God, turn this stone into bread." He was saying, "Jesus, prove to me who You are. Prove that You're really the Son of God. Prove that the voice I heard was really true." Jesus wouldn't do it. He answered, "Man doesn't live by bread alone." He was saying, "I don't have anything to prove. I don't need you to be for Me. I don't need your validation. I'm not going to waste my time trying to convince you of who I am." Then the enemy took Jesus to the highest point of the temple. He said it again, "If you are the Son of God, jump from here." Jesus answered, in effect, "Why do I need to show you who I am when you heard My Father announce who I am just forty days ago? If I was His child in the water, then I'm His child in the desert. I don't need to impress you. I'm not going to show off, hoping you'll be convinced of who I am. I have a destiny to fulfill."

One of the tests that Jesus had to pass in the desert was not proving Himself.

As with Jesus, you have nothing to prove. Don't get distracted by the negative chatter, by people who discount you. Don't start competing with someone who's not in your race, trying to outperform or impress them so they'll be for you. You don't need them to be for you.

The enemy wanted Jesus to show off. "Jump so everyone in the temple below will see how powerful You are, see how the angels come to lift You up, so You can impress all these people." Jesus wouldn't use His power for the wrong motives, just to bring attention to Himself, just to show how great He was. Before He was crucified, He said, "I could have called twelve legions of angels down to turn things around, but I'm not living to impress people. I'm not living to prove who I am. I know who I am. I'm living to fulfill My purpose." When your motives are right, and you need favor or a breakthrough, God will step in and make things happen that you couldn't make happen.

Look Out for the Traps

If anyone could have proved something, it was Jesus. He has all-power. He could have shut the enemy up. He could have created a steak dinner in the desert. He could have flown down off the temple like a fighter pilot, with everyone in amazement. He was showing us that we don't need people's validation. You may have the power to prove something—you have the talent and the funds—you could get even, you could show off, you could impress, but you realize it's a distraction. As with Jesus, we're all going to face these tests. Are you going to take the bait and start competing in things that don't matter? Are you going to try to prove your self-worth, try to impress people, so they'll think you're great? Are you going to try to prove your value when your Heavenly Father has already taken care of that? He's already said He's well pleased with you.

> *Are you going to try to prove your self-worth, try to impress people, so they'll think you're great?*

If we would spend the same time pursuing our goals, working on our assignment, and focused on our purpose that we normally spend trying to prove, trying to impress, trying to feel better about ourselves, how much further along would we be? How much more of God's favor would we see? It puts you under a lot of pressure to live in a proving mode. If you fall into that trap, the enemy won't leave you alone. You prove one thing, and he'll come again. "If You won't turn this rock into bread, then at least jump off the temple, at least prove that You're mighty." The enemy tried three times to get Jesus to prove who He was. He kept coming back again and again. You have to be determined and say, "I am not going to give in to the temptation to prove, to compete, to outperform, or to show people that I'm strong enough, smart enough, talented enough. I have nothing to prove."

Many years ago my father wanted to build a new sanctuary. We were in an auditorium that held a thousand people. The church was growing, and we needed a larger place to meet. For several years he had been making plans, trying to save the funds, but he just couldn't get it going. Several of his pastor friends who were much younger than him were building large sanctuaries. When my father would hear what they were doing, he'd get all fired up and try to make it happen. In the back of his mind, he thought, *I can't let them outdo me. I'm getting older. It looks like I'm falling behind.* There was an underlying pressure to try to compete, to keep up, to prove that he was successful, to prove that he wasn't too old. He was tempted to give in to it, but he recognized that wasn't his race. He wasn't competing with them. He didn't have to keep up. He passed the test.

Ask yourself, "Why do I want to accomplish the dream? Why do I want a bigger house? Why do I want the promotion?"

Several years later, everything fell into place. My father built a beautiful, debt-free sanctuary. It's important to keep the right motives. Ask yourself, "Why do I want to accomplish the dream? Why do I want a bigger house? Why do I want the promotion?" If your motives are pure, if your reason is to fulfill your destiny, to help more people, to accomplish your assignment, then God will bless it. But if it's to keep up with your neighbors, to look good in front of your family, to impress the people under you, it's going to be a struggle. God's favor is not for building our ego; it's to build the kingdom.

Advance the Kingdom

When David went out to face Goliath, his brother had just made fun of him. His father didn't think he had what it takes. King Saul thought he was too small and had to have armor. David had all these people who didn't believe in him. But he didn't go out to prove to them who he was, or to prove that he wasn't too small, or to prove that he was anointed to be the next king. It wasn't about proving; it was about fulfilling his purpose. He saw Goliath as someone standing in the way of the Israelites, a giant defying the armies of the living God. If David had gone out just to prove to people who he was, to feed his ego, he wouldn't have seen God's favor. His motives were to advance the kingdom. He wasn't doing it for people's applause or to gain fame and notoriety. He didn't think, *Hey, this is going to make me look good.* It was about honoring God. When you have the right motives, God will take your sling and rock and cause you to defeat a giant. He'll open doors you couldn't open. He'll cause you to look good, to be honored, to be admired. You weren't seeking to try to impress or to outperform someone. You were seeking the kingdom.

If David had gone out just to prove to people who he was, to feed his ego, he wouldn't have seen God's favor.

My question is, How much pressure are you putting on yourself trying to prove, trying to measure up, trying to get validation? This can be a new day. You can finish reading this chapter much lighter. You have nothing to prove. You don't have to keep up with everyone. You're not in competition with others. You don't have to perform better for God to approve you. He's already said, "You are My beloved son, My beloved daughter, in whom I am well pleased." His approval isn't based on what you did or didn't do; it's based on who you are, His child. You're not supposed to live striving, stressed, and competing. Get off that treadmill. It's stealing your joy. Rest in who God made you to be. Run your race, focus on your goals, and keep the right motives. If you do this, I believe and declare that you're going to live freer and see God's favor in greater ways. You will accomplish dreams, overcome obstacles, and become all you were created to be.

CHAPTER TEN

Don't Rely on People

Your worth doesn't come from another person; your value comes from your Creator.

It's great when people believe in us, cheer us on, and make us feel valuable. We love when our spouse compliments us, a friend is there to give encouragement, or our coworker stays late to help us on a project. God uses people to help move us toward our destiny. But here's the key: You can't become so dependent on people that you're getting your worth and value from how they treat you. It's easy to become addicted to compliments, addicted to encouragement, and addicted to others cheering you on. Now you rely on them to keep you feeling good about yourself, to always be there to validate you, to make you feel approved. They've become like a drug to you. If they don't keep you fixed and meet your expectations, you get discouraged, feel inferior, and work overtime to try to win their approval. The problem is, you're trying to get from people what only God can give. Your worth doesn't come from another person; your value comes from your Creator.

If you rely on people, you'll be disappointed. People will let you down, people will get busy and not be there when you need them, and sometimes people will even turn on you. In the Scripture, Peter was Jesus' close friend. They were with each other day and night. But when Jesus needed Peter the most, when He was on trial and about to be crucified, Peter denied that he even knew Christ. Jesus could have been upset and said, "God, I don't understand it. Why wasn't he there for Me?" He could have let it cause Him to miss His destiny. Quit relying on people. What they do or don't do doesn't determine your worth. What they give you or don't give you cannot stop your purpose. God breathed His life into you. He has crowned you with His favor. Quit waiting for people to approve you, and start approving yourself. People may not encourage you, but you can encourage yourself. People may not make you feel special, but you can make yourself feel special. You can say, "I am a child of the Most High God. I am wearing a crown of favor. I am one of a kind. I am a masterpiece."

People may not make you feel special, but you can make yourself feel special.

You'll have better relationships if you start validating yourself. If you're always depending on somebody else for approval, you'll become needy, a burden, and always waiting for other people to keep you fixed. Can I tell you that your friends have enough problems of their own? Your family members have enough issues that they're dealing with to not come home and have to work on you for three hours. That's not only hurting you, but it's unfair to the people God put in your life. They're not responsible for your happiness. They're not responsible to keep you cheered up. Don't put that extra pressure on them. Learn to receive your value from your Heavenly Father. If you're basing your self-worth upon what people give you, then if they change their mind, if they stop doing it, you'll feel devalued. But when you go to God for it, nobody can take it away. It's not dependent on how somebody treats you, how they make you feel, or how many compliments they give you. It's dependent on the fact that you're a child of the Almighty God, and you know He has already approved you. That's where you're getting your value.

You Don't Need Somebody Else's Approval

You may be saying, "My parents didn't raise me right. I didn't have a good childhood. My spouse never compliments me, and my boss doesn't give me the credit I deserve." I say this respectfully: If you didn't get it, you didn't need it. They can't stop your destiny. What they say or do cannot override God's plan for your life. Shake off the negativity. That person who walked away, who did you wrong, who made hurtful comments—shake off the disrespect. Don't believe the lies that you're not talented enough, attractive enough, or good enough. They don't determine your value. They can't lessen your self-worth. The only power that people have over you is the power you give them.

Jesus had all kinds of people come against Him. Politicians, religious leaders, haters, and critics tried to discredit Him, make Him feel inferior, and cause Him to give up. He could have taken the bait and thought, *I must not be very special. Listen to what they're saying about Me. Look at how they're treating Me.* But Jesus understood this principle. He knew His value didn't come from people; it came from His Heavenly Father. In John 5, He said to a group of His critics, "Your approval or disapproval means nothing to Me." He was saying, "I don't need your approval to feel good about Myself.

> *"Your approval or disapproval means nothing to Me."*

I don't have to have your encouragement or support to keep Me moving forward."

The apostle Paul said it this way in the book of Philippians: "I am self-sufficient in Christ's sufficiency." Our sufficiency is not in our own strength, but when we know that the Creator of the universe lives in us, when we know He's equipped us, empowered us, and anointed us, we can put our shoulders back and hold our head high, knowing that if God approves us, we don't have to have people's approval. It's good when people encourage us, when they cheer us on, but what I'm saying is to not become dependent on that. If someone's not giving you what you expect, if they're not validating you, that's okay. You can validate yourself. You can approve yourself. You are self-sufficient in Christ's sufficiency. You can feel good about who you are, knowing that God handpicked you, created you in His image, and put seeds of greatness inside.

You are self-sufficient in Christ's sufficiency.

What am I saying? You don't need somebody else's praise. You don't have to have people's applause. You have the applause from the One who matters most, from the God who spoke worlds into existence. I'd rather have His applause than people's applause. But you may say, "Well, if I could convince this person to like me, he knows a lot of people, and maybe he could open some new doors for me." The Scripture says, "Promotion doesn't come from people. It comes from the Lord." God knows where all the opportunities are. He can make things happen for you without you having to convince someone to like you. You don't have to play up to people, try to win their favor. If they don't want to be your friend, it's their loss and not yours. Do yourself a favor and keep moving forward. They're not a part of your destiny. God has divine connections for you, people He's already lined up. They're already in your future.

People Can't Give What They Don't Have

Sometimes the reason people don't give us what we need is because they don't have it. Nobody gave it to them. They didn't see it modeled when they were growing up. If they weren't raised by parents who showed affection, who expressed feelings of love and were good to each other, the problem is, they don't have it to give. If you're trying to get it from them, you're going to be frustrated. Why don't you let them off the hook and go to God for what they can't give you? Here's the key: God has it all. If you learn this principle of not relying on people, but go to Him for your encouragement, for your approval, for your self-worth, then you won't live stressed out because somebody is not giving you what you expect. If nobody's complimenting you, you can compliment yourself. Get up in the morning, look at yourself in the mirror, and say, "Good morning, you good-looking thing." Call it by faith. God calls you a masterpiece. Say what God says about you. "I am strong. I am healthy. I am one of a kind. I am highly favored."

You have to build yourself up. Encourage yourself. Compliment yourself. You cannot rely on your spouse, your parents, your coach, your teacher, or your pastor. They may mean well, and they couldn't love you more than they do, but no person can meet all your needs. Only God can. If you're just looking to people, eventually you're going to be resentful, bitter, and start holding it against them. It will sour the relationship. The truth is, it's not their fault. Maybe they have their own issues; they could be doing better in areas. If you don't rely on people but instead go to God, you won't be dependent on what somebody does. If they're not giving you what you need, and that was the only way to get it, they would control your destiny. God didn't design the plan for your life and say, "Okay, it's all dependent upon whether or not

You have to build yourself up. Encourage yourself. Compliment yourself.

these other people do right. If they encourage you, if they cheer you on, and if they never let you down, you will reach your destiny." No, God put everything you need within your power.

Instead of living needy, thinking, *Why don't they compliment me? Why won't they be my friend?* the right attitude is, *Nobody owes me anything. I don't have to have people's approval, applause, or compliments. I know where to go for everything I need. I am self-sufficient in Christ's sufficiency.*

Change Your Perspective

My father was raised in poverty on a cotton farm during the Great Depression. He didn't have enough food, hardly any clothes, and only received a limited education. He had a very rough childhood. At the age of seventeen, my dad gave his life to Christ, and he left the farm and went out and started ministering. Years later, when he was in his forties and had become a successful minister, he started thinking about how he was raised and all the things he'd had to endure. He wondered why his parents didn't give him a better childhood, why he had to go without food and without a good education. All these negative memories filled his mind, and he started thinking, *That wasn't right. They should have done better. They didn't give me what I needed.* He got so stirred up about it that he was about to travel back to his parents' home, confront them about it, and tell them what he thought.

Just before my father was going to get in the car, he heard a voice inside saying, "They did you wrong, didn't they?" He said, "Yes, they sure did." The voice continued, "It wasn't fair, was it? They didn't give you what you needed." He answered, "No, it wasn't fair." "You're going to let them have it." "Yes, I'm going to let them have it." Then the voice said, "How do you think you would have done if you had been in their shoes? How would you have done with no income, with the banks closing, with nobody to buy the cotton, with six children to feed and raise, and with no electricity, no washing machine, and no modern-day conveniences?" That conversation changed my father's perspective. He realized that his parents did the best they could with what they had. They couldn't give him what they didn't have. Why don't you let the people in your life off the hook as my father did? Maybe they did the best they could. They may have made decisions that you don't understand, decisions that you feel put you at a disadvantage, but you didn't have to walk in their shoes. Maybe nobody gave them what they needed to give to you. The bottom line is, nobody owes you anything.

God is keeping all the records. He has seen everything that's happened in your life—the injustice, the bad breaks, the person who did you wrong. Those people cannot pay you back. They cannot make you whole. Only God can. He said He will give you beauty for ashes. He said He will pay you back double for the unfair things that have happened. Quit looking to people to make it up to you. Quit trying to get somebody to apologize, to admit they were wrong, to give you what they don't have. If you go to God, He'll bring you out better. He'll make the rest of your life more rewarding and more fulfilling than if it hadn't happened in the first place. That's what my father did. He let it go. He realized his parents couldn't give him what they didn't have. Daddy went on to live a blessed, prosperous, successful life.

Those people cannot pay you back. They cannot make you whole.

No Person Can Meet Your Needs

When you let people off the hook and quit trying to make them perform perfectly and keep you fixed, not only will their life be better, but your relationships will improve. No matter how good a person is, they can't give you everything you need. I realize I can't meet every need that Victoria has. I can encourage her, compliment her, and treat her with respect. I can do my best, but I'm human. I have flaws and shortcomings. If she looks to me alone, she'll be disappointed. But if you look to God, you'll never be disappointed. No person has 100 percent. I've heard it said that in a relationship the most the other person will have is 80 percent of what you need. There will always be 20 percent they cannot give you. The mistake we make is when we leave the 80 to go find the 20 in somebody else. The problem is, that next person will be missing 20 percent as well. If you're a husband, you may be thinking, *Joel, my wife is missing a lot more than twenty percent.* Think of it this way: If she had more, she wouldn't have married you!

Part of the 20 percent that Victoria needs but I'm missing is that I don't like to talk a lot. People see me on television and think I'm outgoing, but in private I'm quieter and reserved. Small talk is not one of my favorite things. And, yes, at home we talk and laugh and have fun together, but Victoria and her family can talk for hours. They enjoy one another. We had lunch one time at our house with all her family, and after about thirty minutes, when I had finished eating, I asked to be excused and went to the back room to watch the football game. Three and a half hours later, I came back and they were still sitting at the table. Nobody had moved. I was so amazed. I asked them, "Did you all go somewhere?" Victoria said, "No, we didn't go anywhere." I said, "What are you talking about?" Victoria said, "Nothing." They talk about nothing longer than anybody I know.

The key to a good relationship is to recognize the other person's strengths and weaknesses, then give them room to be who they are. Don't try to squeeze them into your mold. One thing I appreciate about Victoria is that she doesn't say, "Joel, come in here and talk with us for three and a half hours or I'm going to get upset. I'll give you the cold shoulder." She recognizes that's a part of the 20 percent that I don't have. I thank God every day that I didn't get it. But Victoria doesn't try to squeeze me into her mold, and even more importantly, she doesn't try to get something from me that I don't have. If you're relying on another person to meet all your needs and become everything in your life, you're going to become disappointed. Let them off the hook.

Don't try to squeeze them into your mold.

Quit Trying to Please People

Sometimes God will let us go through seasons when we're not getting what we expect from people. On purpose, He'll have them withhold it to teach us to not rely on another person, but to get our encouragement, our value, our worth from Him. I mentioned earlier that when I first started ministering back in 1999, I was very insecure and unsure of myself. I had never done it. My dad had a heart attack and went to be with the Lord, and I stepped up to pastor the church. I was so concerned about what people thought—was I doing it good enough, were they going to accept me? After the services when I'd talk with visitors and different people, I lived off the compliments of the people who had good things to say. "Joel, that was good today. I really enjoyed it." Those comments were like water to my thirsty soul. I was getting my approval and validation from people. God can use that to get us going and keep us moving forward for a while, but at some point, as a mother weans a baby off a bottle so the child can grow up, God is going to wean us off our dependence upon people's compliments and applause. It doesn't mean it's never going to happen, but it means you're going to get to the place where you're not dependent on someone else cheering you on so you can feel good about yourself. You're not dependent on them complimenting you and keeping you encouraged. It's nice to hear, but you've developed a self-sufficiency. You don't rely on people for their approval; you go to God for your approval.

The first year I started ministering at Lakewood, people cheered for me every time I got up to speak. They were very encouraging, very loyal and supportive. Every time I walked off the platform, Victoria would say, "Joel, that was amazing today. You did so well." It might have been the worst message in the world, but I could always count on her to tell me it was good. I know sometimes she was lying, but I needed it back then. This went on for about a year, then one day after I had finished my message and walked off the platform, Victoria didn't say a word. I stood there and waited and waited, gave her plenty of opportunities, but still nothing. I thought, *Well, she's just preoccupied, thinking about something else.* I went out to the lobby to talk with the visitors, but not one person complimented me on my sermon. Usually every other person would say something, even if they were just being polite. I thought they were playing a trick on me. I left the church so discouraged. When I got home, my little dog who is always waiting at the back door, so happy to see me, jumping up on me, wasn't even at the door. I walked over, and she was in her bed. She looked up at me, barely opening her eyes as though to say, "Oh, it's just you." Then she closed her eyes and went back to sleep. God will even use your dog to work on you.

Looking back now, I realize that God was teaching me to not rely on what people think, to not have to have their applause and approval. He was weaning me off those compliments. If I had not learned that back then, I wouldn't be where I am today. I've learned that the higher God takes you, the more disapproval, the more opposition, and the more critics you'll have. If you're basing your worth and value on how people are treating you, on how much they're cheering you on, and you're trying to keep them happy, you'll never become everything God created you to be. In those early years, if I heard one negative comment it would ruin my whole Sunday. I would go home discouraged, thinking that I wasn't good enough. But now that I've been weaned off that bottle, so to speak, if I hear something negative, it doesn't bother me. I realize that as long as I'm doing my best, honoring God, I don't need people's approval. I have Almighty God's approval.

If you're basing your worth and value on how people are treating you, on how much they're cheering you on, and you're trying to keep them happy, you'll never become everything God created you to be.

You're never going to keep everyone happy. Quit trying to please people. When you come to the end of life, you're not going to stand before people and give an account; you're going to stand before God. He's not going to ask, "Did you keep everyone happy? Did you please all your family? Did you have the support from your coworkers?" He's going to ask, "Did you fulfill My purpose for your life? Did you run your race? Did you finish your assignment?" As with me, maybe you're not getting from people what you once did—the compliments, the support, the encouragement. Instead of being frustrated, have a new perspective. God is growing you up. He's getting you prepared for the next level of your destiny. The less you depend on people, the stronger your spiritual muscles are going to become, the happier you're going to become, and the higher you're going to go.

Less Is Better

In Judges 7, after the Midianites joined forces with two other armies, they crossed the Jordan River and were about to attack the Israelites. When Gideon sent messengers out to gather men for war, thirty-two thousand Israeli warriors showed up ready to fight. Gideon was feeling good. He had an army that he felt was adequate to protect the people of Israel. But as they marched out toward the enemies, God said to him, "Gideon, you have too many people with you. If you win the battle, the Israelites will think they did it in their own strength." God instructed him to tell everyone who was fearful and afraid that they could go home. Twenty-two thousand men turned around and left. He instantly lost two-thirds of his army. I'm sure Gideon gulped and said, "God, did You see what just happened?" God said, "Yes, I saw it. But Gideon, you still have too many people." God told Gideon to take the remaining ten thousand men down to the stream to get a drink and divide them into two groups. Every man who knelt down and drank with his mouth in the stream was put in one group. The second group was made up of the men who cupped the water in their hands and lapped it up with their tongues like dogs. Nine thousand and seven hundred men put their mouth in the stream. That was the group that was to go home. Only three hundred men drank from their hands. His army went from thirty-two thousand to three hundred.

I can imagine that Gideon thought, *God, I was confident with thirty-two thousand. I was a little worried with ten thousand, but three hundred men? This is impossible.* God was saying, "Gideon, you don't need everyone you think you need. You're depending on too many people." God is saying this to us: "You don't need all your coworkers to support you. You don't have to have all your friends and family members cheering you on." Here's the key: The less you depend on people, the greater the anointing on your life. When you're not depending on someone else, hoping that they'll help you, thinking that they're the Savior, then God will release His favor in your life in a greater way. Gideon went out with those three hundred men, just one percent of what he started with, and God supernaturally helped them to defeat the armies that were much bigger and much better equipped.

The less you depend on people, the greater the anointing on your life.

In the same way, God is going to give you victories where the odds are totally against you. You think you can accomplish your goal if you just have the support and the connections. You think you can overcome that obstacle if you have the strongest players, the best people on your legal team. God is saying, "Don't worry about it. You don't have to have all those people." You and God are a majority. The forces for you are greater than the forces against you. Now quit saying, "Oh, if they'd just train me, if they'd just get behind me." If you quit depending on people, the anointing will increase in your own life. You will accomplish more with less help and fewer people and live more fulfilled because of God's favor on your life.

Are you frustrated because you don't think you have enough support? Have this new perspective: The greatest force in the universe is breathing in your direction right now. Are you discouraged because people are not giving you what they once did? It's because God is growing you up. Quit trying to get from people what only God can give. Go to Him for your value, your self-worth, and your encouragement. If you start passing these tests as Gideon did, not relying on people, you'll not only live more peaceful, more confident, and more secure, but you're going to overcome obstacles that look insurmountable and accomplish dreams that seem impossible.

CHAPTER ELEVEN

Be Comfortable Not Knowing

Don't let what you don't know and what you can't see keep you from releasing your faith.

We all have situations that we don't see how they're going to work out. We study the facts, the numbers, the reports, and the odds are against us. We do our best to come up with a plan, to find a solution. We think we have to have the answer or it's not going to happen. But there are some things that God doesn't want us to know. He has the solution, but if He showed you right now, it wouldn't take any faith. If you could see how your child is going to turn out and the doors He's going to open, the provision, the healing, and the favor, it would be easy to believe. The test comes when we don't have the answers, when we don't see how it could happen. Thoughts tell us, *How are you going to make it financially after you retire? What if you don't get the scholarship? What if your health doesn't improve?* The problem is that sometimes there is no logical solution. The more we try to reason it out, the more discouraged we get, and we start thinking, *What am I going to do?* This is what faith is all about. You have to be comfortable not knowing. You don't have to figure it out and come up with a plan. It's okay to not know.

When Moses led the two million Israelites out of slavery into the desert and toward the Promised Land, they were excited. God had just delivered them from Pharaoh after hundreds of years of captivity in Egypt. I can imagine them asking Moses, "Where are we going to camp in the desert?" Moses answered, "I don't know." "Where are we going to get food?" "I don't know." "Where is the water supply?" "I don't know." "How are we going to protect ourselves?" "I don't know." "What route are we going to take?" "I don't know." They could have said, "Moses, what kind of leader are you?" But just because you don't know doesn't mean God doesn't have a plan. Moses was comfortable not knowing. He had such a trust in God that he didn't have to understand how everything was going to work out. He didn't have to have all the details. He took it one step of faith at a time. Sometimes we think it's a lack of faith to say "I don't know." We think we have to have all the answers, have it all figured out. Take the pressure off. You don't have to know; God knows. He has you in the palms of His hands. He's directing your steps.

Just because you don't know doesn't mean God doesn't have a plan.

The Scripture says that God has planned out all of your days. He has a blueprint for your life, but there's a catch. He doesn't show you all the details. If He showed you what He has in store, where He's taking you, it would excite you, and you would be amazed. But when you saw what it's going to take to get you there—the giants you're going to have to face, the lonely nights, the betrayals, the closed doors, the Pharaohs who will stand in your way—you would think, *No, thanks, God. I'll just stay where I am.* One reason that God doesn't show us the answer is that He knows we would talk ourselves out of it. If you can't figure out how something is going to work out, and you start getting worried, losing sleep, wondering what's going to happen, that's a sign that God doesn't want you to know. You have to be comfortable not knowing.

> *One reason that God doesn't show us the answer is that He knows we would talk ourselves out of it.*

Faith says, "God, I don't know how I'm going to raise these children, but I'm not going to live worried and stressed out. I don't know how my business is going to make it, but I trust You when I don't have the answer. I don't see how my family can be restored, but I trust You when I don't see a way. I realize I don't have to know because You know, and You control the universe." That attitude of faith is what allows God to do great things, to make ways where you don't see a way. The fact is that He had the solution before you had the problem. He could show you how it's going to be resolved. He could give you all the details, but if He's not, then it's a test. He doesn't want you to know right now. Will you be comfortable not knowing? Will you trust Him when you don't see how it can happen?

It's Okay to Not Know

I'm the type of person who wants to know. I like to have a plan. I'm always trying to figure things out. When I didn't see a way, I used to get stressed. I was tempted to worry, to live on edge. It's very freeing when you learn this principle that there are some things we're not supposed to know. It's okay to say as Moses did, "I don't know how it's going to work out, but I'm at peace." That's not a lack of faith; it's just the opposite. You're taking yourself

That's not a lack of faith; it's just the opposite. You're taking yourself off the throne and putting God on the throne.

off the throne and putting God on the throne. When we're trying to figure everything out, to come up with our plan, and we're thinking, *If I can just make this happen. Maybe I can manipulate this situation and convince this person to like me*, we're being God. As long as you're on the throne, God will step back. But you have to learn to say, "God, I don't see how this can work out, but I'm not going to worry. I'm not going to spend all my time trying to fix something that only You can fix. I trust You. I know Your plans for me are for good." When you're comfortable not knowing, God will get you to where you're supposed to be.

When you're comfortable not knowing, God will get you to where you're supposed to be.

When we acquired the Compaq Center, it was going to take a hundred million dollars to renovate it. We had to build our own power plant and air-conditioning system. When I looked at it on paper, there was no way we could raise the funds in the scheduled period of time. We analyzed it and did projections, and even in the best-case scenarios, we were still millions short. Every day I was tempted to worry. Every day thoughts said, *What are you going to do? It's not going to work out.* We had already signed for the loan and construction had started. Right before we moved in, we were scheduled to make a large payment, millions of dollars. We didn't have it, and there wasn't any sign that we would get it. The closer that date came, the more pressure I felt.

When I was tempted to be stressed, I would always come back to the fact that I knew God had given us this building. I would say,

"God, I saw You change city council members' minds to vote for us when they were against us. I know it was Your favor that opened this door, and I know You didn't bring us this far to leave us. I don't see how it can happen, but I'm okay with not knowing how, because I know You are still on the throne." Two weeks before the big payment was due, we unexpectedly got the opportunity to sell a piece of property. We were told it would sell for a certain price, but it sold for almost twice that amount. It was the hand of God moving at just the right time, making a way where we hadn't seen a way.

You may have some things you don't understand, you can't figure out, and you don't see an answer. That's okay. You don't have to see it. Don't get discouraged, and don't start complaining. God is working behind the scenes. He's about to make things happen that you didn't see coming. It's going to be out of the ordinary, unusual. You're going to know it is the goodness of God. Moses didn't have all the answers. He didn't know how the Israelites would make it through the desert, but God gave them manna to eat each morning, something like bread that formed on the ground. He brought water out of a rock—unusual, uncommon. He guided them with a cloud during the day and a pillar of fire at night. He brought the walls of Jericho down, not by them fighting, not by their own effort, but simply by the Israelites marching around the walls. They experienced supernatural protection and supernatural provision. Just because you don't have the answer doesn't mean God is not going to show up and do amazing things.

Just because you don't have the answer doesn't mean God is not going to show up and do amazing things.

Your Faith Will Be Tested

My challenge is that you trust Him when you don't understand, that you be comfortable not knowing. The writer of Proverbs says, "Trust in the Lord with all your heart, and lean not to your own understanding." Take this in the right way, but there are times when you have to turn your mind off. Don't try to figure everything out. Use common sense and be wise, but when you start getting frustrated because you can't find a solution, when you're tempted to live worried, that's a sign that God doesn't want you to know.

My father pastored Lakewood for forty years. He didn't raise up a successor as many churches do. He didn't appoint a committee to search for the next pastor. Deep down, I believe he knew what was going to happen. He always wanted our family to take over, but nothing formal was put in place. When he was in his seventies, people would ask him who was going to take over at Lakewood, what was going to happen when he passed. He always told them, "I don't know what's going to happen, but I do know that God is not going to let it go down." He told people, "It's not my church; it's God's church." I'm all for having structure and plans in place, but God's ways are not our ways. God doesn't do it the same way every time. Sometimes God doesn't want you to know. It's a test of your faith. Will you trust Him, or will you live worried, stressed, wondering how it's going to work out?

When my father died, I had only ministered one time, which was the week before he passed. But when he went to be with the Lord, I knew I was supposed to step up and pastor the church. I had never had the desire before, but suddenly God put the desire in me. If my father had tried to make me the pastor before he died, I wouldn't have done it. What happens the normal way may not be

God's plan for you. God didn't show my father who the next pastor was to be. My father could have lived frustrated and tried to make something happen, but instead he was comfortable not knowing. He knew God was in control. He trusted His plan. Just because God doesn't show you the future doesn't mean it's not going to work out better than you can imagine. I'm sure my father is looking down from heaven and saying, "Look what the Lord has done." It's more than he ever dreamed.

Just because God doesn't show you the future doesn't mean it's not going to work out better than you can imagine.

When you're comfortable not knowing, it will save you so much stress and worry. If you can't figure it out, it's because God doesn't want you to figure it out. He doesn't want you to know now. You can analyze the situation, try to reason it out, worry for six months, and nothing's going to change. It's so much better to say, "I don't have the answer, but I'm okay because I know that God has the answer."

"I Know Not, but I Do Know..."

The apostle Paul says in Romans 8, "We know not what to pray." Here's a man who wrote almost half the books of the New Testament, one of the most brilliant minds of his day. Yet he says, "We know not." He was comfortable with what he didn't know. He didn't see it as a lack of faith to admit, "I don't have all the answers. I don't know what to pray all the time. I have uncertainties, things I don't understand, things I'm not sure how they're going to work out." The reason he could say this and not be worried or become bitter and ask, "God, why did this happen to me? Why is it taking so long?" is found two verses later. He says in verse 26 that "we know not," then in verse 28 he says, "We know that all things work together for good to those who love God." The way you can say "we know not" and not be worried is if you know all things are working for your good. "I know not how it's going to work out, but I do know who's on the throne. I do know who's directing my steps. I do know who's planned out my days for good." Are you frustrated by what you don't know, what you can't figure out, what doesn't look as though it's going to work? Have a new perspective. Even the apostle Paul said he didn't know. It's okay to not have the answers.

> *The way you can say "we know not" and not be worried is if you know all things are working for your good.*

In Acts 16, Paul and Silas were in prison. They had been out sharing the good news in the city of Philippi, hadn't done anything wrong, but the opposition stirred up trouble and had them arrested, then severely beaten with rods. They were put in the deepest part of the dungeon with their feet chained to the stocks. They didn't know if they would ever get out, if they would have a fair trial, or if they would be put to death as the apostle James had been previously killed by King Herod in Jerusalem. They had all kinds of questions to which they didn't have answers. Their situation was out of their control. I'm sure thoughts were telling them, *This is not going to turn out well. You've seen your best days.* They could have been upset and worried. But at midnight, instead of complaining, they were singing praises and giving thanks to God. Their attitude was: *We know not how this is going to work out, but we know God is in control. People can't stop our destiny. God being for us is more than the world being against us.*

As they were singing praises, suddenly there was a great earthquake, the prison doors flung open, and the chains fell off their feet. They walked out as free men. You may not know how your situation can work out, the odds are against you, you've gone through all the options, come up with all the scenarios you can think of, but nothing works. You could live worried and upset. No, be still and know that He is God. You don't have to be God. You don't have to figure it out. You don't have to come up with the solution. God is on the throne. The reason you can't figure it out is because we think natural, but God is supernatural. He's about to make things happen that are out of the ordinary, things that we can't see.

Be still and know that He is God. You don't have to be God. You don't have to figure it out.

It's very powerful when you can say, "I know not what's going to happen with my health, but I know that God is on the throne. I know not how my child is going to get on course, but I know that God is fighting my battles. I know not where the money is coming from, but I know that God's plans for me are for good and what He started in my life, He will finish." You don't have to know how as long as you know who is in control of your life. That's when the Creator of the universe will open doors you couldn't open, break chains that have held you back, bring dreams to pass that seemed impossible. When you "know not," don't live worried. Do as Paul and Silas did and keep thanking God that He's working, keep talking like it's on the way, keep a song of praise in your heart, keep being good to people, keep doing the right thing. Don't let what you don't know and what you can't see keep you from releasing your faith.

"What Are You Going to Do?"

When we face a challenge and don't see an answer, many times there's a voice constantly whispering, "What are you going to do? What are you going to do?" That's trying to pressure you, to get you uptight, to get you to worry. When you understand that you don't need to have the answer, that it's not your job to figure it out, and you're comfortable not knowing, it takes the pressure off. If somebody says to you, "I heard about your problem. What are you going to do?" your answer should be, "I don't know, but I know the One who does." It's okay not to know. You have to be at peace with what you know not. You may not have an answer to questions about your health, your marriage, or your finances. You've thought of every option, tried everything you can think of, but you don't see how it can work out. Leave it alone. Quit trying to figure it out. Take the same time that you would normally spend thinking about it, worrying and wondering, and start using it to thank God that He's working. Thank Him that He's making crooked places straight. Thank Him that all things are working for your good. You weren't created to live pressured and worried. Sometimes we bring this on ourselves by trying to change things that we can't control, by trying to figure out something that God doesn't want us to figure out.

Take the same time that you would normally spend thinking about it, worrying and wondering, and start using it to thank God that He's working.

I know a man who was in a legal battle for over ten years that involved the government and several other parties. He had done something in his business that he didn't think was wrong, but these other people had accused him of being dishonest. If the decision didn't turn out in his favor, he would lose his freedom. His case was moving so slowly. For years, when he wasn't at his job, he was working on his case with his team, running every possible scenario. They didn't see how it would resolve in his favor. After about five years of living worried, stressed, not enjoying his family, with that hanging over his head, he finally did what I'm asking you to do. He said, "God, I don't see an answer. There's no logical solution, but I'm not going to worry about it anymore. I'm not going to try to figure it out. I'm turning it over to You."

This man changed his approach. He took himself off the throne and put God back on the throne. Instead of worrying, He started thanking God that He was fighting his battles, thanking Him that what was meant for harm He was turning to his advantage. Five more years went by, then out of the blue, the other party dropped the lawsuit. All the complaints against him were dismissed. He said, "I never fathomed that would happen. That wasn't even an option. I was just hoping I would win at the trial, that God would give me favor with the authorities." But God's ways are better than our ways. What He has in mind is much better than what we have in mind.

God's ways are better than our ways. What He has in mind is much better than what we have in mind.

Don't be discouraged by what you don't see, by what you can't figure out. You don't know what God is up to. He's going to surprise you. Doors are going to open that you never dreamed would open. As with this man, problems suddenly resolve in your favor. The medical report says no way, but God makes a way. You didn't see how you could get out of debt, but an explosive blessing comes—a promotion, a contract, something that thrusts you to a new level.

It's going to be out of the ordinary. That's why you couldn't figure it out. That's why you couldn't find an answer. God is going to do it in a supernatural way. You're going to see the surpassing greatness of His favor, something that you weren't expecting.

Trusting When You Don't Understand

In the Scripture, God told Abraham to leave his country and take his family to a land that He would show him. It's interesting that God didn't tell him where. I can imagine him telling his wife, Sarah, that they were moving. She says, "Oh, great! That's exciting. Where are we going?" He answers, "I don't know." She asks, "What should I wear?" "I don't know." "What's the weather going to be like?" "I don't know." Abraham would never have become the father of our faith if he wasn't comfortable not knowing.

When you study the heroes of faith, you see how often they said "I know not." David said, "I know not how I'm going to defeat this giant. He's twice my size, but I know God is on my side." Esther said, "I know not if the king will accept me without an invitation, but I'm going to take this step of faith, believing that God has chosen me to save my nation." Joseph, left by his brothers to die and sitting in a pit, said, "I know not how I'm going to lead a nation as God showed me in the dreams, but I trust His plan." The way they stayed in faith was knowing that all things were working for their good. Even when they didn't have answers, they trusted that God was in control.

> *The way they stayed in faith was knowing that all things were working for their good.*

God gave Abraham the promise that he and Sarah would have a baby when they were way too old. Years passed with no sign of the child. Every circumstance said it was impossible, but Abraham understood this principle. He said, in effect, "We know not how it can happen, and there's no way in the natural, but we trust You, God. We believe that what You promised will come to pass." Sarah had a baby when she was ninety years old. God did what they never dreamed could be done.

When that little child, Isaac, grew to a young man, God told Abraham to take him up a mountain and sacrifice him. They traveled for three days and finally arrived. Isaac said, "Dad, we have the wood, and we have the fire, but where is the lamb for sacrifice?" Abraham said, "God Himself will provide." It didn't make sense that God would give Abraham a son, the child for whom they had waited so long, and now He was telling him to take his life. Abraham didn't understand it, he was no doubt confused and uncertain, but his attitude was: *God, I don't know what You're doing, but I trust You.*

That's a key to faith: Trusting when you don't understand, trusting when you don't have the answers, trusting when it seems as though it's just the opposite of what you were hoping. That's when it's easy to live worried and frustrated, thinking it's never going to work out. *I don't see how it can happen.* Not knowing is a test. What you do when you don't know, when it looks impossible, will determine what God does. Abraham was about to sacrifice his son when the angel of the Lord called out to him and stopped him. Abraham looked up and saw a ram caught in the thicket. Rams don't normally come up that high on the mountain. Abraham took the ram and sacrificed it. He named that place Jehovah Jireh, which means "the Lord our provider."

When you pass the test of not knowing, God has provision coming, things that you couldn't make happen. You may be where Abraham was. God's promised you something, but it's been a long time, and it seems as though it's too late. You don't see how you could have that baby, how you could get well, how you could accomplish your dream. Stay in faith. You don't have to have all the answers. Not seeing a way doesn't mean God is not going to do it. What He's spoken over your life is still on the way. Like that ram that was way up on the mountain, God has provision coming for you, something that wouldn't have normally happened, something out of the ordinary—favor, healing, the right people, opportunity.

When you pass the test of not knowing, God has provision coming, things that you couldn't make happen.

Because you trust Him when you don't understand, because you're comfortable not knowing, God is going to do things in your life that you can't explain. It might be a promotion that you didn't work for, having a baby when you were told it wasn't possible, getting well when the medical report said you were done, seeing your family restored, or starting a business. What was that? The ram in the thicket. When you obey without the details, when you stay in faith when you don't have the answers, when you believe when every thought says there's no way, as with Abraham, God will show out in your life. He'll cause you to defy the odds and go places you couldn't go on your own.

I'm asking you to be comfortable not knowing. Quit being worried over what you can't figure out. God has you in the palms of His hands. There will be times when you say, "I know not." But don't stop there. Go on two more verses and agree with the apostle Paul and say, "I know all things are working together for my good." If you do that, I believe and declare that you're going to see supernatural provision, protection, healing, and restoration. You'll be happier, and you will be free to fulfill what God has planned for you. God is going to not just bring promises to pass, not just turn problems around, but it's going to turn out better than you ever imagined.

CHAPTER TWELVE

Win the War Within

Don't keep giving in to the same things that you know are holding you back.

There's a battle taking place inside each of us. It's a battle between the flesh and the Spirit. The flesh represents our carnal nature, and it shows out in ways such as jealousy, pride, and compromise. It's the easy way to live. You don't have to be disciplined; you just do whatever you feel like doing. If someone is rude to you, you're rude back to them. If you don't feel like having a good attitude, you go through the day sour. When you see the coconut cream pie on the kitchen counter, you don't think twice about having a fourth piece. The flesh wants to rule; it wants to have control. In Romans 8, the apostle Paul says, "Those who live by the dictates of the flesh." Notice that he describes the flesh as a dictator. What do dictators do? They make all the decisions for you. They tell you what to do and when to do it. You just follow orders. If you get stuck in traffic, the flesh will tell you, "Get upset. This is ruining your day." Many people follow the dictates of the flesh like good soldiers and say, "Yes, sir. Right away." They get upset, and it sours their day. When they get to the office, a coworker leaves them out of a meeting. The flesh says, "Get offended. This is not right." They go around offended, with a chip on their shoulder.

The problem is, if you keep giving in to the flesh, Paul goes on to say, "You will die." That doesn't mean to die physically, but your dreams will die, your relationships won't flourish, and your gifts won't come out as they should. What's the problem? You're letting the flesh win the war. Anytime you're tempted to compromise, to be lazy, to give in to temptation, there's another option—to walk in the Spirit. That means you do the right thing when it's hard. You bite your tongue when someone is rude. You stay faithful in your relationship when someone is trying to lure you away.

Anytime you're tempted to compromise, to be lazy, to give in to temptation, there's another option—to walk in the Spirit.

What's limiting some people is not that they're not talented or that they don't have God's favor. It's that they keep sowing to the flesh. Don't keep giving in to the same things that you know are holding you back. The next time that you're tempted to be jealous, to find fault, or to say something critical, tell your flesh, "No, I'm not going there. I'm going to be happy for them. I'm going to see the best in people." When you feel like staying up and playing on the computer all night, tell your flesh, "Not tonight. I'm going to bed. I'm going to take care of myself." The next time the friends who are pulling you down and causing you to compromise want to get together, tell them, "Sorry, something has come up. I can't hang out tonight." Quit letting the flesh be the dictator. You have to take charge of your life. The flesh is not leading you anywhere productive.

Dethrone the Flesh

Paul says in Galatians 5, "The flesh desires what is contrary to the Spirit, and the Spirit what is contrary to the flesh. They are constantly fighting each other. Your choices will never be free from this conflict." I don't want to depress you, but this is a battle that will never go away. You can be a believer for fifty years, you've grown and matured, but you will still have to deal with the flesh. You don't overcome it one time and it's gone forever. It will come back again. This is something we have to get skilled at doing over and over. "No, I'm not going to do what my flesh says it wants. No, I'm not going to take the bait and get offended by the person who did me wrong. I'm not going to let my guard down and be dishonest in this business deal." Are you winning the war within? Are you living by the Spirit, making decisions that honor God, or are you letting the flesh win, doing whatever you feel? You need to take the flesh off the throne. Quit letting it determine your decisions.

Are you living by the Spirit, making decisions that honor God, or are you letting the flesh win, doing whatever you feel?

In countries that are ruled by a dictator, we have seen the person in charge oppressing the people, pushing them down. There's no democracy. Because they can't vote him out, and because he won't change, the people often have to take drastic measures, rising up and overthrowing the dictator. They have to forcefully remove him. That's the only way they can be free. It's the same way with the flesh. It wants to stay in control of your life, telling you what to do and where to go. The only way it's going to come off the throne is if you forcefully remove it. It's not going to go easily. When someone does you wrong and you choose to forgive, the flesh will have a fit. "Come on! Get even. Pay them back. This is not right." You have to put your foot down and say, "Sorry, but you don't control me anymore. I've taken you off the throne. You've lost your authority. I walk by the Spirit and not by the flesh." It's time to dethrone the flesh. Quit letting it dictate how you live, how you respond, how you handle adversity. Start sowing to the Spirit. Start taking the high road, doing the right thing when it's hard. That's when you grow. That's when God can trust you with more. It's very shallow to live by how you feel, giving in to carnal desires. That's going to keep you from the greatness God put in you.

The Scripture says, "No discipline at the time seems pleasant, but later on you will reap a harvest of good things." Being disciplined is not easy. Walking away when someone is rude, not giving in to a temptation, and getting up early to excel at work are difficult. Your flesh wants to be comfortable. Your flesh wants the easy way out, but you can't be comfortable all the time and reach your destiny. If you do the hard thing now, later on you'll see blessings and favor that you've never seen. But the flesh always wants instant gratification. "If I tell this person off, it will make me feel good right now. If I buy this item that I can't afford, or if I sleep in and skip work, I'll feel good right now." But it's important to think about later on. We should be growing. We should be getting stronger. We should be further now than we were five years ago. If I'm still dealing with my temper the same way I did years ago, I'm leaving my flesh on the throne. If I'm still getting offended, upset, and jealous in the same way as years ago, I'm letting the flesh dictate my life. I'm not saying we have to be perfect, but we should be growing.

Your flesh wants the easy way out, but you can't be comfortable all the time and reach your destiny.

It's a Daily Battle

When Victoria and I were first married and we were about to go somewhere, I would ask her if she was ready. She'd say, "Yes, I'm ready." So I would get in the car and wait. I'd wait and wait and wait. She would never come. I would get stressed, go back in, and say, "I thought you said you're ready." She'd reply, "I am ready." I would ask, "Well, would you mind coming to the car?" I didn't like to wait. I used to pray, "God, You have to change her. Help her to go faster." But what's funny is that God never changed her, but He used her to change me. God doesn't remove everything that's uncomfortable. If He did, we would never grow. Instead of praying that God will change the other person, I've learned to pray, "God, change me. Help me to come up higher. Help me to be more patient. Help me to stay in peace."

Even now, when I get stuck in traffic or in a long line at the airport, that impatience still tries to get back on the throne. It still tries to dictate my life. You won't win the war within one time, and then you're done. These forces are constantly opposing each other. That's why the apostle Paul said to the Corinthians, "I die daily." Now Paul is one of the heroes of faith, one of the most influential leaders of the early church, the most prolific writer of the New Testament. You would think he was so powerful and mature that he wouldn't have to deal with these issues, yet he said, "Every day I have to take my flesh off the throne. Every day I have to put down carnal desires."

You won't win the war within one time, and then you're done.

After a couple of years of being impatient, letting things frustrate me, I tried a different tactic. When Victoria says she's ready, I consider it like the two-minute warning before the end of a football game. The clock says two minutes, but you know that with the time-outs, the replays, and the commercials, it's going to be twenty minutes. Now when she says she's ready, I go sit down, or make a sandwich, or work out, or go to the grocery store, or mow the lawn. I changed my response. Many of the things that frustrate us are really opportunities to grow. You have to take the flesh off the throne. Don't respond the same way you've been responding for the last twenty years. If you just keep being impatient, unhappy, and arguing with your spouse over and over, start dying daily. As with Paul, we all have areas where we're letting the flesh dictate. If we would start walking by the Spirit, being willing to be uncomfortable, to keep our mouth closed, to wait with a good attitude, that's when we're growing. That's when God can trust you with more influence, more favor, more resources. I know there are a lot of battles on the outside, but my question today is, Are you winning the war within? Are you walking by the Spirit and not the flesh?

Put Off the Old Man

When you gave your life to Christ, when you were born again, the Scripture says, "You became a new creation; the old things have passed away." I would love to tell you that means you'll never have any more carnal desires, that you'll never want to be jealous, rude, or complain. No, the old man may have died, but I've learned a secret. Sometimes he'll be resurrected. Lazarus wasn't the only one who came back to life. Your old nature will rise from the dead.

Lazarus wasn't the only one who came back to life. Your old nature will rise from the dead.

Ephesians 4 says, "Put off the old man and put on the new man." Even though you're a new creation, you have to put off the old. Every day that old man is trying to get back up and run your life.

We see this with Peter. He was a faithful disciple, strong and committed. Jesus said, "You are Peter, and on this rock I will build My church." God had great confidence in Peter. When the soldiers came to arrest Jesus, Peter was so determined to stand up for Jesus that he pulled out his sword and cut off the ear of the servant of the highest priest. But just hours later, when Jesus was taken to the high priest's house to be tried, Peter denied that he knew Jesus before two girls. Then when others gathered there and said, "You're one of His disciples, too," Peter got angry and started cursing. "What are you talking about? I don't know the man." As with Peter, we all have the old man and the new man inside. That's why the Scripture says to put off the old man, put off the pride, put off the bitterness, put off the compromise, and put on the new man.

"Joel, I'm trying, but I can't control my temper. I can't break this addiction. I can't keep my eyes on the right things." Quit telling yourself that. Your old man is not that strong. The reason he's controlling you is that you keep feeding him. Whatever you feed is going to grow. Every time you give in to that temptation, you're feeding it. It's getting stronger. Every time you're offended, you're impatient, or you say things you shouldn't, you're feeding the negative. Do yourself a favor and quit feeding the old man. If you start starving the bitterness, starving the jealousy, and starving the compromise, it will get weaker and weaker. That desire may not totally go away. God may not totally remove it. This is when discipline steps in. This is when His grace shows up. Don't use the excuse: "I've tried, and nothing

If you start starving the bitterness, starving the jealousy, and starving the compromise, it will get weaker and weaker.

has changed." You have the power to overcome. Every time you resist a temptation, every time you make a better choice, you will get stronger, and it will get easier. Don't let that old man get back up. I still deal with being impatient. That old man has been trying to get back up for forty years. I buried him, had a funeral, thought he was finished, but you've heard of the walking dead. Sometimes he gets back up.

Here's what I've learned. Anything you defeat quickly is not your real enemy. You don't have to be concerned with what you overcome in a short time. Your real enemy doesn't go away overnight. I'm not tempted to be dishonest, curse, or do drugs. By the grace of God, those things are not a struggle for me. But being impatient is a different story. David defeated Goliath in a few minutes. That wasn't his real enemy. King Saul tried to kill David for many years. He threw spears at David in the palace and chased him through the desert. God could have delivered David from Saul in a moment, as He did with Goliath. He could have taken care of Saul in an afternoon. Saul was no big deal. But God doesn't remove some enemies, some temptations, some desires. It may not go away. If God doesn't remove it, that means His grace and power are there to help you stand strong and deal with it.

God wouldn't have allowed it if it was going to keep you from your destiny. Ask Him to help you. Ask for His strength. When you admit your dependence on Him, you humble yourself and say, "God, I can't do this on my own. I can't defeat this giant. It's not going away." Then God will step in and help you conquer what's holding you back. You have the power to keep the old man down. Don't let him keep you from your greatness. Don't let the flesh stay on the throne. The force in you is greater than any force that's trying to stop you. Start putting on the new man. "Father, thank You that I

You have the power to keep the old man down.

am strong, I am disciplined, I am anointed, I am favored, and that I make decisions that honor You."

Put on the New You

In Chapter Six, I described in detail how a man named Nabal insulted and deeply offended David, and how David and his men would have killed every male in Nabal's household had not Nabal's wife, Abigail, intervened and kept David from carrying out vengeance. Abigail described her husband as a fool. The Scripture says that he was rude, harsh, hot-tempered, hardheaded, dishonest, ungrateful, disrespectful, and that he spent most of his life drunk.

It's interesting that Abigail was the opposite of her husband. She was not only beautiful in body and spirit, but she was very wise. When she and her servants met David and his armed forces with a large provision of food and wine, she bowed down in humility and apologized for Nabal's offense. She calmed David down and kept him from making a mistake that would have impacted his destiny. David thanked her and turned around and went back home. Ten days later, Nabal had a stroke and died. David sent word and asked Abigail to become his wife. Now that the old man was dead, she could meet the new man.

Nabal is symbolic of our old nature—hot-tempered, rude, ungrateful, stuck in addictions. The name *Nabal* even means "fool." As long as the old man is alive in us, we'll never meet the new man. The old man is seen in bitterness, bad attitudes, and compromises. Start starving the old man. Your destiny is too great, your assignment is too important, to let the same issues keep you from seeing the new man. It's interesting that Nabal died ten days after Abigail did the right thing. There will be these times when you dig down deep and do the right thing when it's hard, and you will come into your tenth day and something will suddenly break. That addiction won't have the power over you. That bad attitude and temper may not totally go away, but it doesn't control you anymore.

I wonder how much higher we would go if we would start putting off the old man. How much more of God's favor would we see if we would start saying no to the things that are holding us back? Sometimes a little thing is keeping us from big blessings. It may be a little pride or a little compromise. "I just have this one friend I still party with. It's just this one temptation I give in to. I just have this one person I won't forgive." No, it's time to get rid of Nabal. Nobody likes him. Nobody wants to be around him. Put the old man down and put on the new you—the free you, the blessed you, the happy you, the victorious you.

> *How much more of God's favor would we see if we would start saying no to the things that are holding us back?*

Be Israel, Not Jacob

In the Scripture, Jacob was known for being dishonest, for cheating people. His name means "deceiver, trickster, con man." He lived up to it. He tricked his father into giving him the family blessing rather than giving it to his firstborn brother, Esau, and he went around deceiving people. After living this way for many years, he decided to return to his father's home and face up to his wrongs. On the way, one night he went down to a brook alone.

I'm sure he was reflecting on his life. It was there that he had an encounter with God, and God changed his name from Jacob to Israel. His new name means "prince with God," and his old name meant "deceiver." He spent the rest of his life dealing with these two names. From this time on, you would think the Scripture would only refer to him by his new name, Israel. After all, God changed his name. It was a significant moment. He had a new beginning. But the Scripture goes back and forth between naming him Jacob and Israel. One moment he's Jacob, yet a few verses later he's Israel. God was showing us that the old man, the carnal desires, won't totally go away. The key to living in victory is to respond as Israel, not as Jacob. There's a Jacob in all of us. There are things that can hold us back. The good news is that there's an Israel in all of us. There's a prince in you. There's a holy, righteous, favored, world changer in you.

There's a prince in you. There's a holy, righteous, favored, world changer in you.

Let me warn you that even though Israel is in there, even though God has changed your name, Jacob will try to come out. Those carnal desires may be dead, but people will do things that wake up the Jacob in you. You'll be driving to work, singing praises, enjoying the day, and Israel is feeling good. Then someone cuts you off in traffic. Out of nowhere, Jacob shows up. You quit praising, and you start saying some other things. You think, *Jacob, where did you come from?* Jacob smiles and says, "I'm in here, too. I may be dead, but I can be woken up." Jacob wants to complain; Israel wants to praise. Who's going to win that war? Jacob wants to hold a grudge and says, "They hurt you. Don't speak to them." Israel wants to forgive and says, "Let it go. Move forward in faith." Jacob wants to argue, be condescending, and say hurtful things. Israel wants to be kind, overlook the offense, and keep peace in the relationship.

Jacob wants another Krispy Kreme doughnut, with chocolate icing and sprinkles on top. Israel says, "No, twelve was enough."

Jacob wants another Krispy Kreme doughnut, with chocolate icing and sprinkles on top. Israel says, "No, twelve was enough." I'm asking you to be the Israel, not the Jacob. They're both in us. God changed your name, but he didn't get rid of Jacob.

At the end of Jacob's life, when he was about to pass, the Scripture says, "When Jacob was told, 'Your son Joseph has come to you,' Israel gathered up his strength and sat up in the bed." He started off as Jacob—tired, weary, thinking he was done—but then something kicked in. He thought, *Joseph, my son whom I thought was dead, the one I waited for, is here. I'm not going to die yet.* Israel sat up. The prince in him came back to life.

When you wake up in the morning, you get to choose: "Am I going to be Jacob today? Am I going to complain, not want to go to work, get upset in traffic, and let people get on my nerves all day?" Or are you going to be Israel? "Lord, thank You for another day You have made. I'm grateful to be alive. Thank You for the gift of this day." When things don't go your way, when you have delays, disappointments, and people do you wrong, are you going to be Jacob? Are you going to get upset, be offended, and try to pay them back, or are you going to be Israel? "Father, You are my vindicator. You're on the throne. I'm going to stay in peace, knowing that You are fighting my battles." With your family, are you going to be Jacob—critical, harsh, and contentious? Or are you going to be Israel—loving, kind, and treating them with respect and honor? Both the old man and the new man are in you, the flesh in conflict with the Spirit, Jacob and Israel. You'll go so much further in life if you start being Israel. Keep the flesh off the throne. Don't let that old man get back up. Keep him buried.

Let the Spirit Rule

I was at a drive-through recently, just minding my own business. Life was good. I had waited about ten minutes in line. I pulled up to place my order on the microphone, but there was no window to see the customer service people who were inside the building. As I rolled down my window, a man's voice came through the speaker in an irritated tone and said, "Sir, there are other people waiting! If you don't place your order, you're going to have to get out of line." I had just pulled up. I had not been there for two seconds. Out of nowhere, Jacob showed up. I was so surprised. I said, "How did you get here so fast?" He replied, "I live here, too." Jacob then gave me some great ideas of what to tell the jerk…I mean the man. I said, "Jacob, I thought you were dead." He answered, "I was, but I got back up for this one." At that moment, I had to make the choice: Was I going to be Israel, the pastor with a smile, or was I going to be Jacob and try to get even? I did what I'm asking you to do. I thought, *I'm going to be Israel.* I said very politely, "No problem. Let me give you my order." After I ordered, I thanked him and said, "God bless you. Have a great day. I hope your children are fine, and tell your grandparents I said hello." When I pulled up to the window, he had all his coworkers gathered around, staring at me. He said, "I thought that was you, Pastor Joel." I wanted to say, "Yes, this is me, Israel."

Every day you have to make the choice: "Am I Jacob, or am I Israel? Am I going to hold on to this offense, or am I going to let it go? Am I going to hang out with the friends who cause me to compromise, or am I going to stay on the high road and be a person of excellence? Am I going to cut corners at work, or am I going to have integrity and give it my best?" I'm asking you to be an Israel. Put off the old man. Don't let the flesh dictate your

The choices you make don't just affect you; they affect your children and even generations to come.

life. Let the Spirit rule. Honor God with your decisions. The choices you make don't just affect you; they affect your children and even generations to come. Jacob's brother, Esau, sold his birthright for a pot of stew. He was so hungry that he let his carnal desires dictate his decision. As the firstborn son, he sold something incredibly valuable for a bowl of stew. We should talk about "the God of Abraham, Isaac, and Esau," not "and Jacob." But Esau let his flesh take the throne. Don't let that be you.

You can win the war within. God is calling you higher. Whatever you know is holding you back, this is the time to make a change. This is a moment of grace to do what you couldn't do before. Your decision can save your marriage. It can take you to a new level in your career. It can break mediocrity and launch you into abundance. If you do this, I believe and declare that you're going to break bad habits, resist temptation, and become the prince you were created to be, as Israel did.

CHAPTER THIRTEEN

Tame the Tongue

Words can leave scars. Words can tear people apart.

One reason people get stuck in life is because they haven't learned to control their mouth. They say hurtful things, they put people down, and they argue. They don't realize their mouth is keeping them from rising higher. God won't promote you if you don't have the character to back it up. You don't have to be perfect, but you should always be improving. You shouldn't be where you were five years ago. Pay attention to what you're saying. Sometimes our words have been harsh, sarcastic, and condescending for so long that we don't even realize it. We may not be aware that we're saying things to please our flesh rather than choosing to exercise the fruits of the spirit. Your friends may not tell you this, but they don't like it. Your coworkers won't say anything, but they'll distance themselves from you. You'll run off good people because your tongue is untamed.

The apostle Paul said to the Ephesians, "Let no unwholesome talk come out of your mouths, but only what is beneficial to the progress of others." Before you say something, you need to ask yourself, "Is this comment going to be beneficial to somebody else? Is it going to build them up or put them down? Is this comment going to make my spouse feel better about themself, or is it just going to feed my ego?" These are tests that you have to pass. The only thing that's holding some people back from a healthy marriage, good friendships, or a promotion is their tongue. They're talented, they're skilled, but they pop off, they're sarcastic, and they stir up strife.

You can't say everything you feel. Your emotions will get you into trouble. When somebody gets on your nerves, irritates you, and you feel annoyed, instead of popping off and saying things you'll regret later, step back, take a deep breath, and pause for thirty seconds. Think about what you're going to say. Don't speak out of your emotions. Don't let your tongue run wild. That's the easy way out. You have to be disciplined and tame your tongue. The Scripture says, "Be quick to listen and slow to speak" (James 1:19). If you pause for a moment and let your emotions calm down, you'll make better decisions. Some things are better left unsaid. You don't have to win every argument. You don't have to comment on every situation. You don't have to set everyone straight. They may be wrong, and you know you're right, but you have to ask yourself, "Is this worth starting a fight over?" Just bite your tongue and let it go. I've heard it said that the reason we have two ears and one mouth is because we're supposed to listen twice as much as we speak.

Don't speak out of your emotions. Don't let your tongue run wild.

Zip It Up

Do you know how many headaches you could save yourself from if you would just zip it up? In the heat of the battle, it's easy to make hurtful comments that you're going to regret later. It takes ten seconds to say it, but the pain is still being felt ten years later. It's like the burn mark left behind on the skin after a fire has long since died out. We can apologize and say we're sorry, which is the right thing to do, but it doesn't take away the scar. It doesn't make the pain go away. It's much better to tame the tongue, to be slow to speak, to think about what we're going to say, and to not speak out of emotions. This does so much damage to our relationships. We've heard the saying, "Sticks and stones may break my bones, but words will never hurt me," but that's not true. Words can leave scars. Words can tear people apart. Words can make them feel insecure, inferior, not valuable. There are people today who are not reaching their potential because of hurtful words that were spoken over them. They heard their parents say over and over, "You're not that smart. You can't do anything right." Or their spouse is always condescending toward them. "You're so slow. You're unattractive. You're not talented." Now those words are limiting that spouse's future.

> *Words can leave scars. Words can tear people apart.*

David prayed in Psalm 64, "Protect me from the sharp tongues of the people who wield them as swords." He referred to hurtful words as swords. Are you building people up with your words, or are you cutting people up with your words? Are you encouraging them, making them stronger and more confident, or are you putting them down, leaving them wounded and scarred? Many times we can recover from a physical wound much quicker than an emotional wound.

> *Are you building people up with your words, or are you cutting people up with your words?*

As parents, we have a responsibility to speak words of life, faith, and encouragement into our children. Yes, we have to correct them, but don't do it in an angry, disrespectful way. Don't say derogatory things that are going to damage their self-esteem. With a small child, you shouldn't tell them, "You're a bad boy. You're a bad girl." Don't get that down in their spirit. Your child is good. They're made in the image of God. He breathed life into them. They may have bad behavior, but they are good. Correct them in love, with a kind spirit. Don't start cutting them up at an early age with negative, hurtful words. They have enough to overcome in life as it is. They have enough people and circumstances coming against them. Let's be parents who speak words of life that push our children into their destiny and help release their dreams. God has entrusted us with our children. They are a gift from God. With that gift comes a great responsibility. God is counting on you to guide them, nurture them, and encourage them to become who they were created to be.

It All Starts at Home

Taming the tongue starts at home. Husbands, make sure you're treating your wife with respect and honor. If you're saying hurtful, demeaning things, putting her down, you're really putting yourself down. You're not just hurting her, you're hurting you. The Scripture says that your prayers won't be answered if you're not treating your wife right. You won't reach your dreams or accomplish your goals if you're cutting her up. I read a study that said one of the main reasons women fall into depression is because they don't have the blessing from their husband. They don't feel valued and appreciated. I know men who treat strangers better than they treat their wives. They're kind and gracious to coworkers, but they're condescending and sarcastic to their spouse.

Jesus says, "You must give an account for every idle word you speak." An idle word means a negative, discouraging, condescending, hurtful word. You've heard the saying, "Always make your words sweet, for one day you're going to have to eat them." When we come to the end of life, God is going to ask, "What did you do with the spouse I gave you? Did you help them to grow, to become more confident? Did you encourage them to stretch to the next level?" If your spouse is not better than when you met them, if they're not more confident and shining brighter, you need to step it up a notch. Check up on what you're saying. Are you speaking blessings? Every time you tell your wife, "You're beautiful," you're causing her to come up higher. She shines a little bit brighter. Every time you say, "I love you. I'm so glad you're mine," not only is your marriage getting stronger, but she's getting stronger. When you encourage her in her dreams, speak life into her destiny, and challenge her to rise higher, you are blessing her future.

> *If your spouse is not better than when you met them, if they're not more confident and shining brighter, you need to step it up a notch.*

Tell your child, "I'm proud of you. I'm blessed that you're mine. You're going to do great things." Those aren't just nice words; those are seeds that will move them toward their purpose. If you had to give an account now for your spouse, for your children, or for your friends, are they better off today than they were five years ago? Are they happier, stronger, more confident, and more successful? If not, you need to make some changes. God gave them to you. He's expecting you to give them back better. After being married to Victoria for thirty-five years, I would be embarrassed to tell you,

"She's not as happy as she was before we met. She's not as confident. She's not as successful. She doesn't feel as attractive." Here's the key: That would not be her fault; that would be my fault. As her husband, I'm responsible to push her forward. I'm supposed to keep her encouraged, strong, and excited.

The Scripture says, "The wife is a reflection of the husband's glory." If your wife isn't shining because you're harsh, critical, and condescending, that's not only making her look bad, that's making you look bad. When some people have to give an account for their words, it will be a sad day. God will look at their spouse, their children, and their friends and see the wounds. He'll see the cuts from sarcasm, the cuts from disrespect, the cuts from condescending remarks. Don't let that be you. Use your words to bless people. Use your words to put people on their feet, to make them feel better about themselves.

When some people have to give an account for their words, it will be a sad day.

Walk Away and Avoid the Fight

In relationships, we all have conflicts and things we don't like. I'm not saying you should never have a disagreement, tension, or stress. I'm saying that you should step back and not make hurtful comments in the heat of the moment. That's going to damage your relationships. "Well, Joel, if my spouse wouldn't push my buttons, and if my children would act right, I wouldn't say things I shouldn't. If my coworkers wouldn't get on my nerves, I'd be more respectful." These are tests that we all have to pass. The people in your life are never going to be perfect. You have to learn to tame your tongue. That means you don't say everything you feel like saying. You may not think it, but you're disciplined enough to zip it up. Maybe your boss is rude to you, and you're about to let him have it, to tell him what you think. The problem is that he's the boss and you're not. After you let your emotions speak, after you give him a piece of your mind, you'll be on a high for about ten minutes, feeling good, giving people high-fives. Then you'll realize that he still has a job and you don't. It's much better to tame your tongue. Then you won't have to live with regrets and ask, "What was I thinking? Why did I say that?"

Love makes allowances for people's weaknesses. Love overlooks a wrong done to us. You have to rise above these petty things that are pulling you apart. Give people room to have a bad day. When they're rude, don't sink to that level. Be an eagle and rise above it. Life is too short for you to live at odds with others, being contentious, arguing over things that don't matter. Some people are so hardheaded that they have to have the last word in every argument. They'll argue for twenty-seven days so they can have the final word. Let it go. Quit wasting your energy. You have a destiny to fulfill. You have an assignment to accomplish. Those are distractions trying to pull you off course. Zip it up and let the other person be right. You may know they're wrong. It doesn't matter. Let them think they're right. Don't waste your valuable time on something that's not moving you toward your purpose.

Give people room to have a bad day. When they're rude, don't sink to that level.

If you argue long enough, you're going to say things that you regret later. A ten-minute argument can set the relationship back ten years. You have to learn to walk away. You're not going to accomplish anything positive in a heated, disrespectful, contentious situation. Let them have the last word, and you keep your peace. You keep your joy. "Joel, that would make me look weak." It's just the opposite. The strongest person is the one who humbles himself or herself and steps back. The Scripture says, "You overcome evil with good." You don't overcome disrespect with more disrespect, insult with added insult, shouting with more shouting. You do it by taking the high road, by being the bigger person, by staying respectful. You don't have to have the last word in the argument. The mature person walks away first. Proverbs 20 says, "Avoiding a fight is a mark of honor." It doesn't say it's a mark of honor to win the fight, to get the last word, or to put the other person down. The honorable thing to do is avoid the fight.

A ten-minute argument can set the relationship back ten years.

In Chapter Eight, I briefly mentioned how when David was a teenager, his father sent him to take a provision of food to his brothers who were serving in the army on the battlefield where it was exciting. David was stuck in the shepherds' fields, taking care of his father's sheep. When David's oldest brother, Eliab, saw David, he was immediately verbally disrespectful toward David and tried to humiliate him in front of some other soldiers. Eliab was trying to start a fight. Some people will make it their agenda to try to bait you into conflict, to stir you up into strife. They can see the favor on your life. They know you're headed for great things. Instead of being happy for you, knowing that God has a destiny for you, they'll be jealous. As with Eliab, they'll try to draw you into battles that don't matter. Don't take the bait.

Some people will make it their agenda to try to bait you into conflict, to stir you up into strife.

I'm sure that David felt like telling his brother off. His

emotions were saying, "Let him have it!" I can imagine David had his speech all lined up. "Eliab, you think you're hot stuff. You're nothing. You're just jealous because I was anointed king and you weren't. You're going to end up serving me." David could have lit into Eliab, but he understood this principle. He didn't get in there and fight. He didn't curse out his brother or try to have the last word. He kept his mouth closed, turned, and walked away. It's no wonder that David took the throne. It's no wonder that God entrusted him to do great things. David had the character to back up the anointing on his life. God can give you a great anointing, He can have a big future in store for you, but if you don't develop your character, you won't step into all that He has. Taming the tongue is a major part of reaching our destiny.

Keep a Seal on Your Lips

Our mouth gets us into more trouble than just about anything else. You can't go around telling people off, using your tongue like a sword, saying hurtful things and pushing people down, and then expect to step into the fullness of what God has for you. Many times it's not big things that are keeping us from God's best. It's not some big sin or some big mistake. It's small things. The apostle Peter says, "If you want to enjoy life and see good things, say nothing evil or hurtful." I wonder how much higher we would go if we would do as David did and not have to have the last word, not have to be right,

I wonder how much higher we would go if we would do as David did and not have to have the last word, not have to be right, not have to make a scene.

not have to make a scene. How much higher would we go if we just keep honoring God quietly, being respectful, staying on the high road?

David faced a lot of opposition in life. He had plenty of opportunities to get upset, to lose his cool, to tell people off. He prayed an interesting prayer in Psalm 141. He didn't ask God to defeat his enemies, and he didn't ask Him to remove all of his difficulties. He says, "Take control of what I say, O Lord, and keep my lips sealed." He was saying, "God, I have a lot of people coming against me, a lot of challenges. I know I'm going to be tempted to say things that I shouldn't. I know I'll be tempted to complain, to argue, to be disrespectful. So, God, I'm asking You in advance to help me zip it up." That's a great prayer. Every morning when we wake up, we should pray, "God, help me to not say things that are going to get me in trouble. Help me to not curse my future, to not be sarcastic, condescending, or argumentative. God, keep my lips sealed."

This is especially important when we face situations that are stressful, when you're dealing with a coworker who gets on your nerves or your child gets in trouble at school. In these pressured situations where you know you're going to be tempted to say things you shouldn't, to blame people, to raise your voice, or to be rude, you need to make up your mind ahead of time that you're going to watch your words carefully. All through the day, say, "Lord, thank You for keeping my lips sealed."

This is what Jesus did. Toward the end of His life, He knew that He was coming into His most difficult season. He knew that He would be betrayed for thirty pieces of silver. He knew He would be arrested, falsely accused and tried in court, and crucified on the cross. He said to His disciples, "I'm not going to be talking with you much more because the prince of this world is coming." He had the wisdom to realize that He was going to be under incredible pressure, so He let them know, "I've already made up My mind that I'm not going to be talking a lot." He was saying, "I've already decided that I'm not going to complain when I'm betrayed. I'm not going to be rude to Judas. I'm not going to argue with the soldiers. I'm not going to be disrespectful to my accusers. I'm going to watch My words carefully."

When you know it's going to be very stressful at work and you're going to be under pressure from your boss, you need to make up your mind before you leave the house: *I'm not going to say everything I feel. I'm going to be extra careful.* When you're going to discuss a sensitive issue with your spouse, determine ahead of time: *I'm going to keep my cool. I'm not going to open the door to strife, arguing, and contention.* If Jesus, the Son of God, who has all-power, said, "I'm not going to talk much in this pressured situation," how much more should we be careful about what we say in pressured times?

If Jesus, the Son of God, who has all-power, said, "I'm not going to talk much in this pressured situation," how much more should we be careful about what we say in pressured times?

Push the Pause Button

It's easy to make excuses. "I was rude because they were rude to me. I said things that I shouldn't have, but I was under so much stress." No, you have the grace to be where you are and not be rude, to not complain, to not say hurtful things. You can either feed your flesh and say what you feel, or you can feed your spirit and keep your mouth closed. If you keep feeding your flesh by saying everything you want, being argumentative and disrespectful, the problem is that you'll never grow. You'll stay a baby. The Scripture says, "Even though you're an heir, even though God has an incredible inheritance that belongs to you—joy, peace, favor, promotion, abundance—if you remain a baby, it won't be released." Taming the tongue is not just about being disciplined; it's about growing up. It's about stepping into your destiny. It's about receiving the inheritance that belongs to you. It's sad to say, but some people are fifty years old and still babies. They haven't learned to tame their tongue. Sometimes we let small things keep us from the big things God has in store. In the big picture, it's a small thing to not argue with your spouse. It's a small thing to not put other people down. It's a small thing to not be sarcastic. God is not asking us to go without food, to give away our belongings, or to move overseas. He's just asking us to tame our tongue. He's asking us to use our words to bless and not curse, to build people up and not tear them down.

This is one reason the Israelites never made it into the Promised Land. God brought them out of slavery in Egypt, and they were headed to the land flowing with milk and honey. But along the way, when they got under pressure, instead of taming their tongues, they started complaining about their conditions. They started criticizing Moses, asking, "Why did you bring us out here in the desert to die?" It was an eleven-day journey to the Promised Land, but because of their negative words, they went around the same wilderness mountain for forty years. That generation of Israelites never made it in. If you're not going to say something good, something beneficial, something that edifies and builds up, do yourself a favor and zip it up. You're not just affecting

If you are critical, harsh, and condescending, you have to take the test again.

the other person, you're keeping yourself from your destiny. God will put us in situations to test us. If you are critical, harsh, and condescending, you have to take the test again. You have to go around the same mountain. Don't do as the Israelites did and go around that mountain for forty years. Start passing the test.

The next time you're tempted to say something you know you shouldn't, put it on pause. Under your breath, say, "God, help me keep my lips sealed. Help me to control my tongue." If you'll be slow to speak and take a moment to ask God to help you, you will start passing these tests. As you grow up, God will release more of your inheritance. You'll see more of His favor. The point is that you can't be critical and still make it into your promised land. You can't be disrespectful to your spouse, your children, or your coworkers and become all you were created to be. You can't talk behind people's backs and reach the fullness of your destiny. This is why Proverbs says, "Life and death are in the power of the tongue." My question is, Are you speaking life into your future, or are you speaking death?

Speak Words of Life

In Numbers 12, Moses' sister, Miriam, didn't like it that Moses had married a woman from a different nationality, a Cushite woman from modern-day Ethiopia. Miriam started talking behind his back, sowing discord, criticizing Moses to her other brother, Aaron. I can just imagine her telling Aaron, "She's not one of us, and she's just after his money. She's just waiting for the movie royalties from *The Ten Commandments*." The Scripture says, "God heard her being disrespectful. He heard her critical, hurtful words." The writer of Proverbs says that God hates when someone is sowing discord, stirring up trouble. All of a sudden Miriam was stricken with leprosy, which is contagious, and her skin became as white as snow. That would seem extreme if she was just talking within her family, but it was going to lead to harmful strife and division among the Israelite people. She had to immediately leave the Israelite camp. Fortunately for Miriam, Moses prayed and asked God to take the leprosy away, and after seven days her skin went back to normal.

It will help us to have the right perspective about our words when we realize that God hears what we say. He hears when we bless people as well as when we curse people. He hears us when we compliment and encourage and push people forward, and He hears when we criticize people and stir up trouble. The prophet Isaiah says that we will eat the fruit of our words. If you sow disrespect, you'll reap disrespect. If you sow sarcasm, discord, and judgment, you're going to reap those same things. But when you sow kindness, encouragement, and mercy, that's what you're going to reap.

It will help us to have the right perspective about our words when we realize that God hears what we say.

Early one morning when our son, Jonathan, was away at college, I sent him a text wishing him a happy birthday and telling him how proud I am of him. Then I went to my office to prepare my message for that weekend. I went over my notes for a couple of hours, and I couldn't get any direction about what I was supposed to speak on. Usually something will jump out at me right at the start, but I just didn't feel it. I didn't have any inspiration, everything felt dull. When I finally came across notes about taming the tongue, I knew that's what I was supposed to share on. About ten minutes later, Jonathan sent me a text back that said, "Thanks,

Dad. You're the best dad in the world." He went on to say some other nice things about me and ended by saying, "I want to be just like you." It's amazing how those few sentences breathed life and energy into my spirit. I felt a lifting, a strength, a joy. I went from being stuck, with nothing coming, and thinking, *This is hard*, to being excited and passionate. Ideas and creativity started flowing, which were all sparked from a few kind words.

James says, "The tongue is like a fire. One spark can set a whole forest on fire." One word can start a major problem, and one word can start a major blessing. I'm asking you to start some good fires. Ignite dreams, ignite hope, ignite passion. Your words can put people on their feet and breathe new life into their dreams. Don't be a part of the problem; be a part of the solution. Be a lifter, be an encourager, be a healer. When you're tempted to say something disrespectful, condescending, or argumentative, be disciplined to zip it up. Put down that sword. Don't go through life cutting people up with hurtful words. Build people up with encouraging words. Every morning ask God to help you keep your lips sealed. If you tame your tongue, I believe and declare you will enjoy your life more, you will have better relationships, and you'll receive your full inheritance.

Start some good fires. Ignite dreams, ignite hope, ignite passion.

CHAPTER FOURTEEN

Living Cause-Driven

The reason some people are not happy and fulfilled is they're ingrown.

There should be something we're involved in that's bigger than ourselves. It's good to have personal goals and dreams, things we want to accomplish. But if you're only focused on yourself, you won't reach your highest potential. You were created to help someone else, to be a blessing, to lift the fallen, to encourage those who are down, to fight for those who can't fight for themselves. You need to have a cause that you're passionate about, some way that you can make the world a better place. It may be to volunteer at a women's shelter, to mentor young men, or to do repairs for elderly neighbors. Maybe your cause is to support great organizations, to help build a children's home, to fund a ministry, or to pay a single mom's rent. The cause may be to break an addiction so your children don't have to deal with it, or to come out of poverty and set a new standard for your family.

When you live cause-driven, you'll do things that you normally wouldn't do. You'll get up early, make sacrifices, and show up when you have other things to do. You're committed to the cause. You don't wake up in the morning and think, *I don't feel like going to work. I don't want to deal with these problems.* Your attitude is: *I'm on a mission. I have an assignment. It's not just about me. Somebody needs what I have and is counting on me. I'm going to be a positive force for good in my neighborhood, in my family, and in my workplace.*

The reason some people are not happy and fulfilled is they're ingrown. As long as you're only focused on you, you're not going to be productive and fulfilled. Look around for ways you can be a blessing. When you give your time, energy, and resources to care for the hurting, to lift those who are disadvantaged, to help bring their dreams to pass, you will see God's favor in new ways. Are you waiting for God to bless you while God is waiting for you to be a blessing? The next level of your destiny is connected to helping someone else.

Are you waiting for God to bless you while God is waiting for you to be a blessing?

"Is There Not a Cause?"

When David was seventeen years old, he was taking care of sheep in the shepherds' fields. It looked as though he was stuck there. He didn't come from an influential family or have an important position. All the circumstances said that he would live an average, ordinary life and never do anything great. One day his father asked him to take a provision of food to his three brothers who were in the army on the battle line with the Philistines. David could have said, "Dad, I don't want to do that. I'm not an errand boy. I'm busy with the sheep. Find somebody else." He could have refused, but this small act of obedience, doing something kind for his brothers, going out of his way to be good to them, is what led to his destiny. Don't discount the small things you can do for people. Bringing someone a cup of coffee, giving them a ride home, making dinner for a neighbor who's not well, and staying late to help train a coworker are small acts of obedience that can lead to big blessings.

Don't discount the small things you can do for people.

When David arrived at the army camp, he heard Goliath, the Philistine giant, taunting the Israelites. For forty days, Goliath had come out twice a day, in the morning and the evening, and shouted threats. When the Israelite soldiers heard them, they were terrified and ran away. But something rose up in David, a holy anger. He said, "Who is this uncircumcised Philistine that he should defy the armies of the living God?" He asked what would be done for the man who killed Goliath. David's oldest brother, Eliab, overheard what he was asking. He was critical of David. He could sense the favor on David's life. He said, "David, why are you even here?" He was saying, "David, you can't do anything about this giant. Look how small you are." David could have been offended and gotten into an argument. Instead, he answered back, "Is there not a cause?" He was saying, "You may be afraid and passive, but this giant is not going to dishonor my God. This is a cause worth fighting for." Something was birthed in David at that moment—a fire, a passion to bring Goliath down.

What took David from the shepherds' fields into his destiny was a cause. He was willing to get involved in something bigger than himself. He didn't have to care about Goliath; he could have dismissed those defiant words. But David stood up for something that in one sense didn't have anything to do with him. He wasn't in the army. Goliath wasn't taunting him. He could have gone back home and lived an average, ordinary life. But when you fight giants for someone else, when you stand up for those who can't stand, you're not just helping them—that cause is going to launch you into your destiny.

When you fight giants for someone else, when you stand up for those who can't stand, you're not just helping them—that cause is going to launch you into your destiny.

David took his sling and slung a stone and defeated Goliath. Eventually he took the throne of Israel. What's interesting is that the crown was in the cause. Without the cause, he would never have become king. As with David, your crown is going to be found in a cause. Your promotion, your breakthrough, and your dream coming to pass are going to be found in being a blessing. Are you fighting for anyone other than yourself? Are you taking risks, stepping out in faith, helping others rise higher? When you're cause-driven, you'll see some giants come down. You'll see promotion, doors open, and the right people show up.

Thousands of Israelite soldiers saw and heard Goliath day after day, but David was the only one who had a cause. He didn't have the size, the training, or the experience, but he believed God was going to show out. He expected to defeat Goliath; he expected to stand victoriously. When you have a cause, you'll believe for big things, you'll pray bold prayers, you'll expect giants to come down.

The Crown Is in the Cause

When the Compaq Center came available as a possible facility for our church, I thought, *God, this is not just about Lakewood. This is about advancing the kingdom. This facility will set a new standard.*

It will be an example of Your greatness. I had a boldness to fight for something way bigger than me. Three years previous to this, I had been running our television production and never pastored, but when you have a cause, you'll believe that you can accomplish what seems impossible, that you can overcome what looks insurmountable. Find your cause. Fight for someone who can't fight for themselves. Get involved in something bigger than you. That's where your crown is. That's where your greatness is going to come out.

Fight for someone who can't fight for themselves.

David could have been satisfied in the shepherds' fields. He could have been satisfied with an ordinary life. "I don't want to get out of my comfort zone. People may criticize me for staying where it's safe, but there are huge giants out there." Safe is not your destiny. Average is not what you're called to be. Take on some giants. Believe to advance the kingdom, to set new standards. God didn't give you the talent, the personality, and the courage you have just to go to work, make a living, and feed your family. You were called for a cause. You are gifted for a cause. You are healthy for a cause. You have influence and are anointed for a cause. Don't just build your kingdom; build God's kingdom. Get involved in making a difference. Where are some giants you can bring down? Where are some people you can lift up? There's nothing worse than to come to the end of life and realize you never saw your crown. You never took your throne. It wasn't in the average or in the routine; it was in the cause. It was in doing something out of the ordinary, getting involved in something that wasn't about you.

Where are some giants you can bring down? Where are some people you can lift up?

It was in making your neighborhood better, blessing a coworker, bringing down a Goliath. That's when you'll see your crown.

I've made up my mind that I'm not going to live comfort-driven. I'm going to live cause-driven. When we're comfort-driven, we don't have to stretch, make sacrifices, take any risks. When I'm comfort-driven, I'm not going to be criticized, talked about, or have opposition. The problem is that you'll never reach your destiny if you live comfort-driven. As long as David was in the shepherds' fields, minding his own business and feeling satisfied, he was average, he was ordinary. Had he not been willing to run that errand to take food to his brothers, he would never have taken the throne. Don't miss the small things. Had he let his oldest brother discourage him, make him upset and bitter, he would have missed his destiny. When he saw Goliath and heard the taunts, if he had thought, *Man, I'd love to help, but I'm afraid. Goliath is twice my size*, he would never have become the king. The cause has to be bigger than the giant. The cause has to be bigger than the opposition, bigger than how you feel.

You may be outnumbered. What you're up against may be stronger and more experienced than you. Don't worry. You and God are a majority. They cannot stand against our God. As with David, there are giants waiting for you. When you defeat them for others, doors to your destiny will open. When you find your cause, the king in you is going to come out. When your dream is connected to helping others, to making your community better, to lifting those who are down, you may think you're just helping them, but what you don't realize is that you're helping yourself.

There are giants waiting for you. When you defeat them for others, doors to your destiny will open.

Find Your Cause

God sees when you serve others and make sacrifices. He sees you helping when nobody is giving you the credit, getting up early to pick up a friend, cooking an extra meal for a neighbor, spending your vacation serving at an orphanage. He sees how you attend and support a ministry, how you volunteer and serve in the community. A lot of times it's on your day off. You could be doing something for yourself, but you're investing in others. Get ready. Your crown is coming. You've been fighting for others; now God is about to fight for you. The king is going to come out of the cause. You're going to see doors open that you never dreamed would open. You're going to see favor, influence, and opportunity, and it's all because you fought for someone else. You got involved in something bigger than yourself.

You've been fighting for others; now God is about to fight for you.

A friend of mine grew up in a small town in Kentucky. His family was poor and they didn't have much. But from the time he was a little boy, he had a desire to help children in need. When he was eight years old, he saw on the television that he could support a hungry child in another country for fifteen dollars a month. He didn't have any money, so he started mowing lawns in the neighborhood in order to help. He needed the funds, but he was living cause-driven, fighting for someone else. When he could have been out playing, he was mowing lawns, making sacrifices for someone he would never meet. That is a nice thing to do, and it's great to be a compassionate person, but it's more than that. When you tap into your cause, there's a crown that's connected.

By the grace of God, my friend was able to attend college.

In the summers, he took overseas trips with doctors to help care for children who were like the children he supported. He ended up going to medical school and beginning his own practice. He became very successful, all the while doing what he could to take care of children. One of his medical suppliers heard how he supported children and asked if he needed anything. The supplier started giving him all kinds of medicines, vaccines, and antibiotics. It grew and grew to where he had to get a warehouse to contain it all. Today, my friends Dr. Todd Price and his wife, Sue, have given over a billion dollars in medical supplies to children around the world. His organization has treated over sixty million children for parasites. He told me that from the time he was a little boy, he always prayed that God would send a wealthy person to help children in need. He said, "I never realized that I would become that person." The Scripture says, "When you help the poor, when you feed the hungry, when you lift the fallen, then your light will break forth like the dawn." Your healing, your abundance, and your breakthrough will come.

Dr. Price didn't have to help those children. He didn't have to take risks, use his vacation time to travel around the world, stay in little villages. He could have enjoyed a nice, average life, but he would never have seen God's favor as he's seen. He would never have been this fulfilled. He discovered the cause was connected to the crown. The cause opened doors to his destiny greater than he ever imagined. I realize that we're not all going to start big organizations or travel around the world helping the needy, but there's someone you

> *There's someone you can fight for, there's something you can do outside yourself that makes your community better, makes your school better, makes your family better.*

can fight for, there's something you can do outside yourself that makes your community better, makes your school better, makes your family better. Find your cause, and you'll find favor and joy.

Be Kingdom-Minded

This is what Nehemiah did. He was a cupbearer to the king of Persia. He wasn't in management and didn't have wealth or influence. He had an ordinary position. When he heard that the walls of Jerusalem had been torn down and the city was unprotected, he was living a thousand miles away. He could have thought, *That's too bad, but it's their problem. I can't do anything about it.* But something came alive inside. He knew that he was supposed to rebuild those walls. How could he do it? He had no money, no staff, no influence, and no experience. But when you're cause-driven, you'll pray bold prayers, you'll believe for the impossible, you'll expect doors to open. I've learned that what God orders, He pays for. When it's to advance the kingdom, when it's to bring about positive change, the resources will be there and the right people will show up. You don't have to figure it all out. All you have to do is believe.

Nehemiah asked the king for permission to return to Jerusalem to rebuild the walls. You can imagine asking your boss for six months off to go do a personal project. You would think the king would say, "Excuse me! You're on my payroll. I need you to be here." But for some reason, the king agreed. He said, "Fine, you can go." As if that wasn't enough, Nehemiah said, "I need another favor. I'm going to need protection. Will you give me a letter addressed to all the governors in the areas I have to travel through, so they won't harm me? And I am going to need timber to rebuild the walls and the gates. I need a letter from you that orders the lumber mills to give me what I need." The Scripture says, "The king granted Nehemiah his requests because the favor of God was on his life." It's good to ask for yourself, but when you're asking for someone else, when you're taking a stand for those who can't, when you're kingdom-minded and not just me-minded, God will show out in your life.

What's holding some people back is that they're only focused on their goals, their dreams, their projects. Why don't you invest some of your time, energy, and resources in someone else? Fight their giants, help their dreams come to pass, mentor their child, or care for them as they go through an illness. That cause is connected to your crown. That's what's going to open new doors to your destiny. Defeating Goliath, someone else's giant, is what took David to the throne. It's good to have your dreams, and it's good to have your goals, but you need to be a part of something bigger than just you. David would have stayed in the shepherds' fields if he hadn't found his cause. Nehemiah would have lived an ordinary life if he hadn't found his cause.

Why don't you invest some of your time, energy, and resources in someone else?

Your Greatness Is About to Come Out

When Nehemiah went to Jerusalem to rebuild the walls, he faced all kinds of opposition. Critics ridiculed and tried to stop him, enemies threatened to attack the workers, and plots were set against his life. It was one thing after another. But when you're cause-driven, you don't go by how you feel. You're not moved by the opposition. You're on a mission; you have an assignment. The cause helps you to stay focused, persistent, and determined. It should have taken Nehemiah years to finish rebuilding the walls, but he did it in just fifty-two days.

I believe there are some Nehemiahs and some Davids who are reading this. You could live an ordinary, average life, but you're fighting for others. You're investing in causes bigger than yourself, making sacrifices to help those around you. You can't help others without God helping you. That cause doesn't come by itself; it's connected to a crown. You're going to see favor, influence, and opportunities that your family has never seen. You're going to come out of ordinary into the uncommon, the unusual, and into resources that you've never imagined. The greatness that God put in you is going to come out of the cause. It's not about finding your crown; it's about finding your cause. Where is a giant that you can defeat, where is a lunch that you can take to your brothers, where is a wall that you can rebuild? If you find the cause, the crown will come.

> *You can't help others without God helping you.*

What's interesting is that the walls of Jerusalem had been destroyed by the king of Babylon over six decades earlier. God could have had a king or a governor or a rich person rebuild them. But God chose a cupbearer, an ordinary person. The cause brought the greatness out of Nehemiah. Without this cause, we wouldn't be talking about him. Without a cause, David wouldn't have become the greatest king who ever lived. I'm asking you to find a cause. Live for something bigger than yourself. The greatness will come out when you help others, when you build their dream, when you support advancing the kingdom. "Joel, I didn't buy this book to be reading about helping others. I want to know how I can be blessed." This is how you'll be blessed. This is how your greatness comes out. This is how you'll discover your crown. "Is there not a cause?"

Invest in Something Bigger Than Yourself

Sometimes the cause is to improve yourself so that your family and those who come after you will be better off. My father was raised very poor. His family lost everything during the Great Depression. He grew up with a poverty mind-set. He wasn't allowed to drink a full glass of milk, just a small portion of milk with mostly water added. But at seventeen years old, he gave his life to Christ, the first person in his family to do so. He felt a calling to become a minister, but his parents tried to discourage him. They told him that all he knew how to do was work on the farm, and that if he left, he wasn't going to make it. The cause has to be louder than the naysayers. What God puts in your heart has to be stronger than the negative chatter. My father made up his mind at the age of seventeen that his children would never be raised in the poverty he was raised in. He had no money, no transportation, and no experience, but he left the farm with a cause.

The cause has to be louder than the naysayers.

He went out and started ministering even though he knew very little about the Bible. He'd only been to church several times. He called Job "job." He preached his first message on Samson, and as he finished he realized that he'd been calling Samson "Tarzan." He didn't have much training, but he had a cause. "I'm going to honor God with my life. I'm going to break this stronghold of poverty. I'm going to set a new standard for my family." He didn't have a ride; he had to hitchhike. He didn't have a church; he preached in prisons and homes for senior citizens. He didn't have an organization supporting him. The first offering he ever received was an apple. There were many times when he was tempted to get discouraged, to feel as though it would never work out, but he would ask himself, "Is there not a cause?" When you live cause-driven, your focus is not on how you feel, not on what people are saying, not on what's not working out. Your focus is on the cause. "I'm not just fighting for me. I'm fighting for my children. I'm fighting to take our family to a new level."

When you live cause-driven, your focus is not on how you feel, not on what people are saying, not on what's not working out.

My father kept going when no doors were opening. He stayed in faith when people were against him. He kept being his best when it was taking longer than he thought. He remained cause-driven, not feeling-driven, not circumstance-driven. As he kept doing the right thing, faithful year after year, he came into his crown. He saw favor as no one in his family had ever seen. He broke the spirit of poverty. God opened big doors. He started and pastored Lakewood for almost forty years, making a great difference with his life. How did he step out of the ordinary into the uncommon? He had a cause bigger than himself. He didn't just think about himself. He thought about his family, he thought about how he could be a blessing to others, and he invested his life in something bigger than himself.

Stay Determined, Stay Focused

Being cause-driven is what's going to help you to stay determined and stay focused. When Jesus was about to be crucified, He didn't feel like going through with it. He was in such distress, so overwhelmed in the garden of Gethsemane that His sweat was like drops of blood. We think He won the victory on Calvary, but really the victory was won in that garden. That's where He made the decision to stick with it. He prayed three times, "Father, if it's possible, let this cup pass from Me." All of His emotions said He should give up. His feelings said He shouldn't go through with it. His mind said that it was not worth it. If He had not lived cause-driven, we wouldn't have salvation. In the darkest moment, He made the decision: "This is not about Me. This is about helping others. This is about fulfilling My purpose." The Scripture says that angels came and ministered to Him in the garden. In those difficult times, when you're trying to break the addiction, trying to keep your marriage together, trying to take your family to a new level, you'll be tempted to think, *It's too hard. It's been too long. This pressure is too much.* When you're in your own garden of Gethsemane, you have to do as Jesus did and make a decision that the cause is worth it.

When you're in your own garden of Gethsemane, you have to do as Jesus did and make a decision that the cause is worth it.

The Scripture says, "Jesus endured the pain of the cross, looking forward to the joy that was coming." Because He was focused on the cause, He was able to endure the pain of the moment. When it's the most difficult, the good news is that you're close to your crown. You're close to your breakthrough. You've come too far to stop now. God didn't bring you here to leave you. Dig down deep. Stay determined. Stay focused. Keep doing the right thing. It's not just for you. You're doing it for your family. You're doing it to advance the kingdom. If you keep fighting for someone else as Jesus did, the angels are going to show up to strengthen you. He sees you giving, helping others, being good to people, taking on their giants. You didn't have to, nobody would have faulted you if you didn't, but as Nehemiah did, you answered the cause, you stepped up to make a difference. Now get ready. The king in you is about to step out. Your crown is about to show up. I believe and declare that you're coming out of the ordinary into the uncommon. God is about to favor you in a new way with promotion, influence, and divine connections. Dreams are coming to pass, addictions being broken, and strongholds are coming down.

CHAPTER FIFTEEN

Take Care of Yourself

I love to say yes, but sometimes to fulfill your destiny you have to say no.

It's easy to get so caught up trying to meet other people's needs and measure up to their expectations that we put ourselves on the back burner. There are the demands at work, pleasing the boss and coworkers. There are family pressures, keeping your spouse happy and raising children, getting one child to football practice and another to dance class. There's running to the grocery store and trying to make the perfect dinner that everyone likes. Then it's off to the neighbor's birthday party. We can't let anyone down. They're counting on us. We develop a hero mentality. We always have to be strong, always be the one who comes through, who cheers everyone else up, who fixes the problems and stays late.

We're doing all these good things to try to keep everyone around us happy. The problem is that we can become depleted, drained, worn-out. We're making sure everyone else is a priority, but we need to make ourselves a priority. Your first mission is to keep yourself healthy and whole. You have a gift. God has entrusted you with talents and dreams. You are valuable. It's not selfish to

Your first mission is to keep yourself healthy and whole.

take time for you. You need time to get refreshed, to be reenergized. You shouldn't be so busy that you don't have time to be alone, or have time to laugh, or have time to exercise. You need recreation. You need these things that help you stay in balance.

When people are making a lot of withdrawals from you, you have to make sure you're putting in a lot of deposits. If you're giving all the time and never filling back up, you're going to be depleted. You're good to others, so why don't you be good to you? You're kind to others, so be kind to you. Be generous to you. Be loving to you. Don't live with a hero mentality that says, "I have to be strong. I have to be at every event. I have to be Supermom who outperforms and overachieves. I can't say no. What will they say if I do?" People will take as much as you give them. They will let you work twenty-four hours a day if you will do it. When you're rundown, emotionally drained, and physically worn out, that's not just doing you a disservice; it's doing your family and those around you a disservice. Not only that, it's not healthy. It's causing you to live overwhelmed and stressed and raising your blood pressure.

Stay in Balance

Nobody can make this change to take care of yourself except you. You have to be the one to say, "I'm going to make some adjustments to my schedule. I'm not going to go running every time this friend calls. I'm not going to live up to pressures and demands that are not reasonable. I'm going to keep myself healthy. I'm going to make sure that I am taking care of my emotional well-being." If you don't learn to say no to some things, nothing will change. The people who are counting on you to perform and always be there for them are not going to say, "Why don't you take a break? Take the evening and spend it doing what you want. I'll cover for you." No, you have them trained. They're expecting you to be there for them. The moment you aren't, they'll say, "What's going on? Where are you, Superman?" You have to tell them, "Superman went to the phone booth and turned back into Clark Kent. Superman was tired. Superman needed rest. Superman had to get back in balance." They may not like it, but your health and emotional well-being are more important than keeping everyone happy.

"Superman went to the phone booth and turned back into Clark Kent."

When you make these adjustments, don't be surprised if you feel guilty and think, *I should be helping. I should be at my neighbor's. I should be working late.* Don't be guilted into doing things that keep you out of balance. There's nothing wrong with taking time for you. When you're tired, you need rest. When you're drained, you need to be replenished. I'm not saying to not work hard. I'm all for working, achieving, and being responsible. What I'm saying is that you need to stay in balance. You can't work all the time, serve your family all the time, and be strong for others all the time. Sometimes you have to say, "Sorry, I need a break. I need a moment to recharge. There have been a lot of withdrawals, and I need to make some deposits."

For me, it's easy to work all the time. It's easy to go ninety to nothing. I like to be productive and achieving something, but I've learned that I'm not as creative if I don't have time for recreation. I'm not as productive if I haven't taken time to laugh with my family, to have fun together, and to exercise. I get refreshed when I work out or play basketball. When Victoria needs to be refreshed, she goes shopping. She'll spend three hours at the mall, never buy a thing, and still be going strong. When I go shopping, I'm drained in five minutes. Everyone is different. Do what replenishes you. Do what brings you back in balance. I know that my brother, Paul, gets refreshed by crocheting.

Everyone is different. Do what replenishes you.

You're Not Superman

When Jesus was on the Earth, He went around healing people, teaching in the synagogues, lifting people up, spending time with His disciples. Everywhere He went, there were needs. People would come up and ask, "Will You heal my child? Will You come to our city? Can I touch the edge of Your robe?" People made constant demands on His time and energies. Imagine how He felt. As the Son of God, He had this incredible power, anointing, and wisdom, so much to offer. Yet at times, when He was tired, the Scripture says that He would go away from the crowds and into the mountains to be alone so He could be refreshed. He could have felt guilty. "There are so many needs. There are people to heal and lepers to cleanse. I can't take a break." But Jesus knew He had to take care of His temple. No matter how anointed you are, you get tired. No matter how strong, smart, or gifted you are, you get depleted. Despite all the needs around you, despite what your children, spouse, boss, and friends are counting on you for, you have to have these times to get alone and recharge your batteries.

If Jesus, the Son of God, had to be alone and rest, if He couldn't meet all the demands of the people around Him, why do we think we can go all the time and be everything for everyone?

"I can't let them down. They're counting on me." I've learned that the sun will still come up if I don't get everything done. The sun will still rise if I don't keep everyone happy. You're not doing yourself any favors if you are living out of a depleted state. Sometimes we've been doing it for so long that we don't realize how far below our potential we're living. You won't be as good a parent, spouse, leader, or friend if you're not taking time to get away. There will always be needs, always be something to do or someone who wants your attention. You have to make it a priority to stay in balance. It's okay to be depleted, to work hard, to give it your best, and to be there for people, but it's not okay to stay depleted. You have to get filled back up. Some people are living worn out, drained, with no energy. They don't want to let anyone down. You've been there for everyone except you. Why don't you treat yourself as good as you treat others? You have to take care of your temple. You're not invincible. Jesus had all the power in the world, yet He knew the limits within His physical body. He knew when He was at the point when He had to take time to get replenished.

If Jesus, the Son of God, had to be alone and rest, if He couldn't meet all the demands of the people around Him, why do we think we can go all the time and be everything for everyone?

The reason some people are not enjoying life is because their account is overdrawn. They're good at letting other people make withdrawals. They work hard, try to meet expectations and keep everyone happy, but they don't have a system whereby they get filled back up. When you live drained and depleted, you won't be as productive. You won't have the stamina to overcome challenges. You won't enjoy your family as you should. There will be more strife and conflict. You'll be amazed at what happens if you get back in balance and make yourself a priority. Let go of some of the pressures. Yes, you love your children, but you don't have to be a super parent. Your children are going to grow up and be out of the house at some point. You don't want to look back and think, *I didn't enjoy those years. I was so stressed and overwhelmed, trying to be everything for them, trying to keep up with my neighbors.* If Jesus knew His limits, we should know our limits. Yes, we can try to do everything. We can try to be Superman, but that's not healthy. Take the cape off. Get back in balance.

You'll be amazed at what happens if you get back in balance and make yourself a priority.

Take Time to Get Replenished

Sometimes it's not other people's expectations that are the problem; it's our own expectations. We feel guilty if we're not doing everything we think needs to be done, if we're not meeting everyone's needs. After all, we think we have the ability, the talent, the anointing. But you also have a physical body. As Jesus showed us, our physical bodies have limits. Jesus had to get away to keep being His best. If He had lived depleted, He would have shortchanged Himself. The best thing He could do was to get recharged. You need to have time on a regular basis where you get replenished. Don't make the mistake of living life with an overdrawn account. If you go into a new week at a deficit, those same things come to take from you, but there's nothing there. That's when you get overwhelmed and frustrated. You're not as productive. Your gifts won't come out as they should. It's not difficult to change it; just get back in balance. On a regular basis, start taking time for you, for what replenishes you, for what fills you back up. This may mean you have to say no to some things. You may have to disappoint a few friends and say, "I can't be there every Monday night. It's a new season." You may have to tell your children, "You can't play on seventeen different soccer teams this fall. You'll have to make do with twelve."

Don't make the mistake of living life with an overdrawn account. If you go into a new week at a deficit, those same things come to take from you, but there's nothing there.

When the pandemic hit, it forced all of us to slow down. Most people didn't go to work or travel. Some of the airlines shut down. Shopping centers closed. Schools went to distance learning. Everything was put on pause. Although there was the tragic loss of so many lives, there was some good that came out of the pandemic. It shifted our priorities. We realized there's more to life than just working all the time, trying to achieve and outperform. We saw how much we missed spending time with our family, enjoying the people we love. In a sense, it helped bring us back into balance, to have a new perspective of what's important in life.

Since 2004, Lakewood has done over two hundred Nights of Hope in cities across America. Every month we traveled to various stadiums and basketball arenas. The events were normally on a Friday night, then we'd come home on Saturday afternoon, do our church service on Saturday night, and two services on Sunday. I write two books a year and do my SiriusXM radio program each week. I love all that I am doing, but I didn't realize how much that was taking out of me. When the pandemic hit, it changed everything. No more events on the road. Instead of three services on a weekend, we recorded one service on Friday afternoon, with no people in the auditorium. I would come in, give my message, and I was done a half hour later. In the twenty-three years since my father passed, I had never been so rested, never had so much energy. I noticed that my eyesight started to get blurry. I couldn't read as well. I went to the eye doctor and he ran the usual tests. He said, "Joel, this is very strange, but the reason your eyesight is blurry is because your vision has improved. It hasn't gotten worse; it's gotten better. You need less correction with your contacts." Who knows what will happen if you get back in balance?

I didn't realize it, but when you have a lot of withdrawals taking place, when you're spending a lot of emotional energy, being productive, seeing your gifts come out, and helping others, you have to make sure you're putting in a lot of deposits. You have to take time to get filled back up emotionally, spiritually, and physically. You may have the drive and the passion to work all the time, but when you do, you're running at a deficit. Your account is low. It starts affecting other things, such as your health, your creativity, your attitudes, your relationships. Stay in balance. Take time to get away. Every day you need to have some time for yourself to get refreshed. Then on a regular basis put on your schedule what fills you back up. Make it a priority to take care of you.

> *You have to take time to get filled back up emotionally, spiritually, and physically.*

You Can Say No

The apostle Paul was supposed to travel to the city of Corinth and visit with the people in the church he had started there. He had told them earlier that in a while he would be coming. They were planning for his visit. But Paul encountered great difficulties in Asia. He had been dealing with problems and people coming against him. He wrote in 2 Corinthians, "We were pressed beyond measure. We were so overwhelmed, we despaired of life itself." This was the apostle Paul, who spent years in missionary travels and planting churches, saying he felt so overwhelmed he didn't think he could go on. It is also clear that Paul's visit with the Corinthians would require additional strength on his part because there were painful problems within the church that needed correction. But he had already told them that he would come. After he made this commitment, these unexpected challenges came up. He could have thought, *I have to keep my word to them. They're expecting me. What if they get upset? What if they don't understand?* But Paul knew his limits. Yes, he was powerful. Yes, he wrote, "I can do all things through Christ." Yes, he prayed and prison doors flung open. But he understood this principle that it was up to him to take care of his physical and emotional well-being. He knew that he couldn't operate at his best if he was depleted, drained, worn-out. So he sent a letter saying, in effect, "I'm sorry that I can't come." He could have had a hero mentality and said, "They're counting on me. I'm the one they look up to. I can't let them down." But he took his cape off and said, "I can't do it." He was saying, "You've seen the superman Paul. Now you're seeing the human Paul. I'm overwhelmed. I have to get replenished, and once I get filled back up and am healthy, whole, and restored, then I'll come visit with you."

There are times you have to be bold as Paul was and say, "No, I can't do it. I know it may hurt some feelings, and I know I've been there in the past. I know I told you I would, but I need a break. I have to get refreshed." Jesus did it, and Paul did it. It's okay if you do it. Don't try to be Superman. Superman is a fictional character.

Jesus did it, and Paul did it. It's okay if you do it.

Superman in real life would have had a nervous breakdown. It's okay to say no. That's one of the most powerful words you can learn to use. I know yes is exciting. We want to do it all. "Yes, I'll work late. Yes, I'll be there for you. Yes, I'll make sacrifices so you can go further." But there will be times when you have to say, "Sorry, but I have to take care of me. I have to protect my health. I have to let my mind rest. I have to release this stress." Sometimes, we're holding on to things that are overwhelming us. What you won't say no to can end up killing you. You've been there for everyone else, so why don't you be there for you? Why don't you make yourself a priority?

I'm not talking about living selfishly. I'm talking about living balanced, recognizing that your physical and emotional well-being is up to you. Some of the people whom you bend over backward for, whom you make great sacrifices to help, are never around when you need help. They're too busy. They have other opportunities. Yes, be good to others, be a blessing whenever you can, but also know your limits. If you can't be a blessing every time, that's okay. If you can't go to Corinth, as Paul couldn't, people may get upset. They may try to make you feel badly, but they're not responsible for your health. They're not going to give an account for your assignment. It's not heroic to try to meet everyone else's expectations and miss your own destiny.

It's not heroic to try to meet everyone else's expectations and miss your own destiny.

A friend of mine was a very successful pastor. He traveled the world helping people and speaking at large events. But he was so caught up in his calling and the doors that were opening that he didn't pay attention to his health. He knew that he was doing too much, running depleted, mentally drained, physically rundown, but he never took time to get replenished. He didn't have a system in place whereby he would get filled back up. You can't keep giving out, letting others make withdrawals, and never making deposits and never putting anything in without hurting yourself. My friend got on an eighteen-hour flight home from overseas. He was so tired, so exhausted. The problem was that he had another trip to take the next afternoon. He told me, "I knew there was no way I could physically do it, but I had this commitment. I wanted to keep my word." He got on that flight and never ministered again. He had a stroke, losing both his speech and motor skills. You're not doing yourself any favors when you're not taking care of yourself. If the apostle Paul can say no, we can say no.

You Make Your Own Schedule

Here's a key: You make your own schedule. You decide what you're going to do. Don't make commitments that you know are not wise for your health. When I get up to speak each weekend, it takes a lot of emotional energy. Physically, I can run all day. But emotionally, there's a limited supply. So on Thursdays and Fridays, I don't schedule any meetings or calls. I know it's going to be a big withdrawal on Sunday, so I have to get filled back up. If I'm dealing with problems during those days, trying to fix situations, plan events, and meet with people, I'm not going to be my best on Sundays. I have to take time to get quiet so I can stay in balance. That's when you're the most creative, the most effective.

There are more demands for your time and attention than ever these days. Everyone wants a piece of you—advertisers, television, the Internet, social media, school, work, family and friends. People are vying for your attention. You have to be selective about what you commit to. When you're at your limit, you can't keep adding to your schedule without taking something else away. We think, *I can go do this, too. My friend wants me to come, and I can squeeze it in. I can write this extra proposal and still make it to my child's tournament.* We have good intentions, but it's too much. If you don't know how to say no, you're going to become overcommitted. It may be for good things, but good things can wear you out. Good people can deplete you. It's all about balance. Does it work with the season you're in right now? Does it fit with what you already have to do?

Good things can wear you out. Good people can deplete you. It's all about balance.

Victoria and I have always loved real estate. If we have time when we see an open house sign, we go in to look around. It's just a hobby. A while ago we were in another state and saw an open house. We went all through the house, and as we were leaving the real estate agent thanked us for coming and asked for my number so he could send me information on other houses. I said, "We're not interested. We're just looking around, not serious buyers." He said, "Okay, but can I get your email address. I'd like to put you on our mailing list." I don't know about you, but I don't need another email, another text, or another phone call. I have enough things already to give my attention to. I said very politely, "No, thanks." He said, "Okay, but at least give me your home address so I can stay in touch." He was very persistent, understandably wanting to make a sale. I'm very nice, and I don't want to hurt people's feelings. Normally, I would have just given in and handed him my brother Paul's email address. But this time I looked at him with a big smile and said, "I'm sorry, but I don't want anyone to contact me." I walked out of there so proud of myself. I had never done that before in my life. I love to say yes, but sometimes to fulfill your destiny you have to say no. The apostle Paul said, "No, I can't come to Corinth right now. I'm too tired." Jesus said, "No, I can't heal people right now. I have to get away and rest." Are there some things you need to say no to? Maybe they're good things but it's not the right season. It's wearing you down, taking time and energy from the main things you need to do.

Are there some things you need to say no to?

Solomon wrote in the Scripture about a woman who said, "My brothers were angry with me; they forced me to care for their vineyards, so I couldn't care for myself—my own vineyard." She was saying, "I've kept everyone else happy. I've met all their demands, worked overtime, built the business, sacrificed for my children, but I didn't take time for me. I didn't keep myself healthy." Don't make the same mistake. You've made others a priority; it's okay to make yourself a priority.

Keep Your Light Shining

Many years ago, there was a lighthouse located on a rocky stretch of coastline. The keeper, who was in charge of keeping the flame burning in the oil lamp, was given a new supply of oil once a month. His main focus was to make sure the lighthouse beacon shone brightly to help sailors guide their ships at night. The lighthouse property was close to a neighborhood. One cold night, an elderly woman came and said she needed oil for her heater. The keeper felt badly for her and gave her some oil. Then a father knocked on the door and said it was an emergency. He needed oil for his lamp so he could travel through the night to get medicine for his child.

The keeper didn't think twice about helping with this good cause and gave him the oil. Another man came saying he was stranded and needed oil to lubricate his wheel. The keeper felt sorry for him and gave him the oil. Toward the end of the month, the supply of oil for the lighthouse was running low. He sent word to town to let them know that he needed more oil. But before the new oil arrived, the oil ran out and the lighthouse beacon went out. That night a huge ship was disoriented in a storm and crashed into the rocks. When the authorities came, the keeper was so apologetic. He told how he'd used the oil to help other people who needed it so badly. They said to him very sternly, "You were given oil for one purpose—to keep the lamp burning and the light shining."

Sometimes we're like this keeper, so good-hearted. We want to help someone, to measure up to their expectations of us, so we run here and there to keep them happy. All the while, we're depleted. Our light is going out. You've been given oil for one purpose—to keep your lamp burning and your light shining, to keep yourself healthy, whole, and strong. If your fire goes out, you can't help others. If you're living depleted, drained, and running on empty, you're not shining as you could. You may be making it, just getting by, but what could you be if you got back in balance. How much brighter, happier, and further along could you be if you do as Jesus did and on a regular basis take time to get refreshed, to be replenished? That means to take care of your temple—physically, spiritually, and emotionally. You're not invincible. Some people may think you're Superman. You're strong, you're gifted, and you always seem to be up. But like the rest of us, you're human. You need to be refreshed.

How much brighter, happier, and further along could you be if you do as Jesus did and on a regular basis take time to get refreshed, to be replenished?

Too many people are burning out. You can go for a while living out of balance, but eventually it will catch up to you. I've heard it said that it's easier to maintain good health than it is to try to regain lost health. When you live depleted, it's wearing you down. It's affecting your immune system. You need to get out from under that pressure. Learn to say no. You may have to stop doing some good things in order to stay healthy. We need you here for a long time. What you have to offer is amazing—your gifts, your talents, your love. Keep your light shining. Yes, be good to others, but don't forget to be good to you. If you do this, I believe and declare that you're going to feel weights lift off you. You're going to live longer, freer, and healthier. You're going to have better relationships, more energy, and become all you were created to be.

Conclusion

I know that the words of this book have fallen on great ground, faithful people. I believe that these words have taken root in the good soil of your heart. My prayer is that you'll see yourself in the way God sees you, as blessed, strong, healthy, full of energy, and full of joy. Start making plans to live a long, healthy life. Things in the spiritual realm have been set in motion in your life, and this is only the beginning.

You can be happier, you can be healthier, you can have better relationships, you can break free from anything that's holding you back, but you have to do your part. It starts when you make plans to live every day joyfully, vibrantly alive, healthy, and productive. Make the decision that you're going to live every day with enthusiasm. Make the decision to go out each day expecting great things, pursuing your God-given dreams.

Every morning when you wake up, think about all the things for which you can be grateful. Start the day with thanks and praise. Start the day in faith. Start the day believing to be your best. Don't drag the past day's negatives into the new day. Release any bitterness, forgive the people who hurt you, and let go of every disappointment. Don't let those toxins build up.

Every day, train your mind to stay at peace. Train your mind to look on the bright side. Train your mind to see the good. Magnify your God and never your problems. Be joyful, laugh often, enjoy even the smallest blessings, and you'll reduce the effects of the day's stress.

Remember that there's nothing more powerful than you making positive declarations over your life. All through the day, keep declaring, "I am blessed. I am prosperous. I am healthy. I am talented. I am creative. I am wise." For a longer and healthier life, I recommend that you make this declaration for life's battles: "I declare God's supernatural favor over my life. What I could not make happen on my own, God will make happen for me. Supernatural opportunities, healing, restoration, and breakthroughs are coming my way. I am getting stronger, healthier, and wiser. I will discover talent that I didn't know I had, and I will accomplish my God-given dream. This is my declaration."

Today is a new day. God is breathing new hope into your heart and new vision into your spirit. He is the glory and the lifter of your head. Look up with a fresh vision, and God will do for you what He promised David. He will put a new song in your heart. You won't drag through life defeated and depressed. You will soar through life full of joy, full of faith, full of victory.

ACKNOWLEDGMENTS

In this book I offer many stories shared with me by friends, members of our congregation, and people I've met around the world. I appreciate and acknowledge their contributions and support. Some of those mentioned in the book are people I have not met personally, and in a few cases, we've changed the names to protect the privacy of individuals. I give honor to all those to whom honor is due. As the son of a church leader and a pastor myself, I've listened to countless sermons and presentations, so in some cases I can't remember the exact source of a story.

I am indebted to the amazing staff of Lakewood Church, the wonderful members of Lakewood who share their stories with me, and those around the world who generously support our ministry and make it possible to bring hope to a world in need. I am grateful to all those who follow our services on television, the Internet, SiriusXM, and through the podcasts. You are all part of our Lakewood family.

I offer special thanks also to all the pastors across the country who are members of our Champions Network.

Once again, I am grateful for a wonderful team of professionals who helped me put this book together for you. Leading them is my FaithWords/Hachette publisher, Daisy Hutton, along with

Patsy Jones and the team at FaithWords. I truly appreciate the editorial contributions of wordsmith Lance Wubbels.

I am grateful also to my literary agents Jan Miller Rich and Shannon Marven at Dupree Miller & Associates.

And last but not least, thanks to my wife, Victoria, and our children, Alexandra and Jonathan and his wife, Sophia, who are my sources of daily inspiration, as well as our closest family members, who serve as day-to-day leaders of our ministry, including my mother, Dodie; my brother, Paul, and his wife, Jennifer; my sister Lisa and her husband, Kevin; and my brother-in-law Don and his wife, Jackelyn.

We Want to Hear from You!

Each week, I close our international television broadcast by giving the audience an opportunity to make Jesus the Lord of their lives. I'd like to extend that same opportunity to you. Are you at peace with God? A void exists in every person's heart that only God can fill. I'm not talking about joining a church or finding religion. I'm talking about finding life and peace and happiness. Would you pray with me today? Just say, "Lord Jesus, I repent of my sins. I ask You to come into my heart. I make You my Lord and Savior."

Friend, if you prayed that simple prayer, I believe you have been "born again." I encourage you to attend a good Bible-based church and keep God in first place in your life. For free information on how you can grow stronger in your spiritual life, please feel free to contact us.

Victoria and I love you, and we'll be praying for you. We're believing for God's best for you, that you will see your dreams come to pass. We'd love to hear from you!

To contact us, write to:

Joel and Victoria Osteen
PO Box #4271
Houston, TX 77210

Or you can reach us online at joelosteen.com.

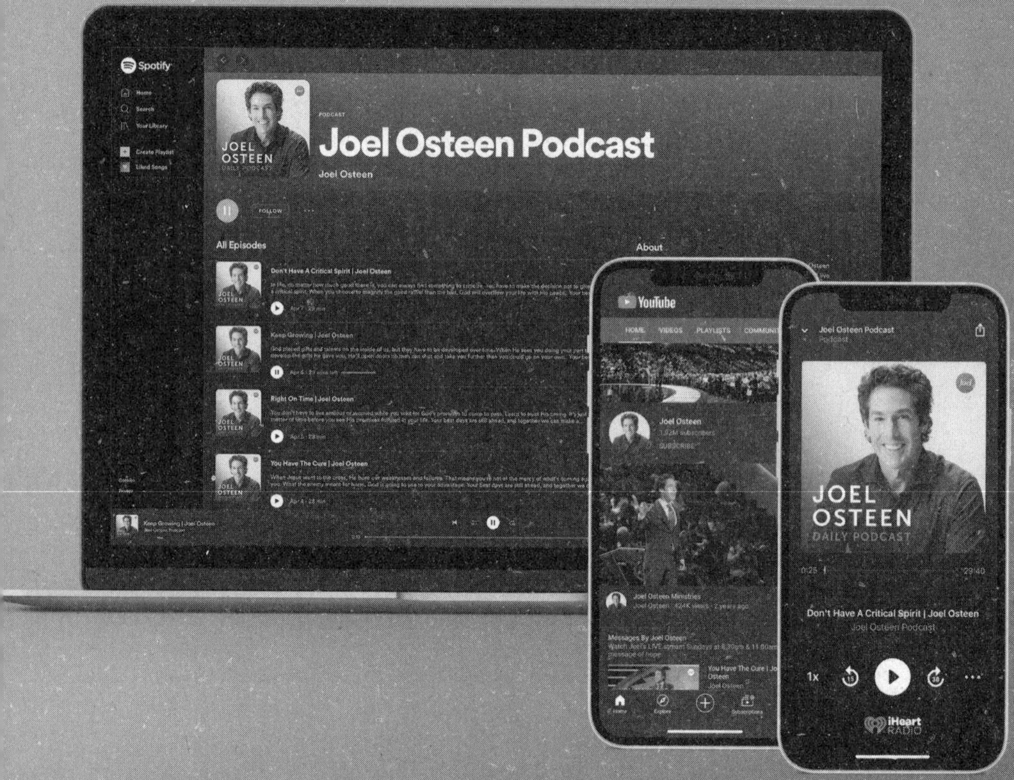